Henry Thomas Hamblin

Achieve Harmony with Cosmic Law

e-artnow 2022

Henry Thomas Hamblin

Achieve Harmony with Cosmic Law

Dynamic Thought & Within You is the Power

e-artnow, 2022
Contact: info@e-artnow.org

ISBN 978-80-273-4290-7

Contents

Dynamic Thought

Things to Observe

Do not worry because you cannot follow the course exactly to the letter. Do what you can of it, adapt it to your life, and do the best you can in present circumstances.

The principal thing is to get twice daily into what is called the Silence, to quieten the senses, and get in touch with the Unseen, i.e., God, Divine Mind, the Infinite, Principle of Good, First Cause, the Absolute, the name does not matter, they all mean the same.

Another vital thing is to use affirmations and denials, these will be explained more fully later.

Yet another is meditation, for you gradually grow into the likeness of that upon which you meditate.

Still another is visualizing. Always visualize the good, the beautiful, and true, and your life will reflect these things. Incidentally, the practice of visualization greatly increases one's powers of concentration.

Also while you are receiving this course and for some time after, refrain from all hazardous speculation. Do not launch out in business without sufficient capital and then expect everything to turn out all right. Instead wait until the way is made clear. Guidance and help will come in time, therefore do not try to force things.

Remember that although as soon as you start right thinking, you begin to build up your life, yet it takes time to manifest. At first things may seem to be worse, if so keep on and they will soon settle down. You cannot fail in the long run if you will persist and persevere.

I want you to realize:

That within you are infinite power and possibilities.

That the inward Power can be aroused and brought into expression by holding high ideals in the mind and by affirmations and meditation.

That it is necessary to spend a short time in the Unseen both night and morning.

That by so doing you can enter a super-conscious realm where your word is creative.

That what you speak comes to pass, that what you mentally picture must come true.

That it is only by following high ideals that true success can be achieved.

Therefore, picture a higher life--the highest you can conceive, and affirm that it is yours. Remember that this higher life is without sickness, disease, forward with joy--you can never fail.

Success and Character Building

PART I

THE objects of this course are: (1) To alter your mental attitude, and (2) To direct your thoughts into those channels which lead to success, achievement, health, happiness and perfect good; (3) The arousing of the inward POWER, and (4) The overcoming of bad habits; (5) The building up of character, and (6) The discovery and development of the creative faculty.

How these are accomplished will be explained to you in their proper place and at the proper time, but first of all I want you to consider, thoughtfully, what is before you. It is not exactly an easy road which you have chosen. No path that leads upward ever is. The path of victory is always thorny; but when the thorns hurt the feet most, we can console ourselves with the thought that the path really does lead somewhere, and we know definitely that it leads to Success, Achievement, Happiness and Satisfaction. Difficulties there will be, disappointments, failures and set-backs, but to him who sets his face towards the light, and will keep steadily onward, there must come success and accomplishment and victory, above all expectation.

If now you merely read this and pass on, the amount of good that it will do you will be none at all. This course is useless if you do not "do" it, reading it will do you little or no good, it is the doing of it that will change your character and your life.

Therefore, stop now and think carefully over the path that lies before you; estimate its difficulties, do not think lightly of them, be prepared for difficulty, and make up your mind, here and now, to conquer.

You may have failed in the past, but this time you must, you will, and you shall overcome every difficulty and weakness, and achieve dominion over yourself, victory over your circumstances and complete control over your life.

> THERE MUST AND SHALL BE NO FAILURE THIS TIME. THIS TIME YOU ARE GOING TO SUCCEED THROUGH THE POWER THAT IS WITHIN YOU.

Now close your eyes, and mentally picture yourself, radiant, strong, successful, happy, full of the joy and zest of life. See yourself treading a path that leads ever upwards. Behind you the air is murky and gloomy, but in front is increasing brightness and loveliness. See yourself progressing, climbing, winning. See yourself trampling old habits and weaknesses under your feet. See yourself meeting difficulties in your path, and see yourself, sustained by a mighty inward power, brushing all obstructions aside, and never faltering in your upward climb.

Concentrate with all your powers upon this mental imagery. Persevere until you can see yourself radiant, sublime, shorn of all weaknesses and imperfections, the perfect image of your perfect self. See yourself full of vitality and health, see yourself successful, attracting both people and affluence to you. Make a concrete, sharply defined image in your mind of yourself as you desire to be; see yourself master of circumstances, attracting all good things by the power of your mental forces.

> WHATEVER YOU CREATE, IN THIS MANNER, IN YOUR MENTAL WORLD, WILL LATER BE MANIFESTED IN YOUR OUTWARD LIFE.

In other words, by mental imagery you are creating your future self. You will gradually grow into the likeness of the image that you are now creating. Therefore create the right image. Let your ambition be a high one; do not picture yourself as a common man, satisfied with vulgar pleasures, instead, create a perfect man, the most perfect of which you can conceive.

In the same way when you throw your mind forward and foresee the task before you and "will" that all difficulties shall be overcome, and that if you get weary of well doing, you will not give up but will persevere, and arouse fresh interest in the task of self culture and achievement, then you are already winning the battle in advance, you are making your ultimate success doubly sure.

I want you to realize that this journey of yours is not a walk over, I want you to understand that it is a fight all the way, but at the same time to realize that it is a winning fight all the time; for although difficulties are real, yet you have within you the Powers which make difficulties and obstacles melt away. Great and omnipotent is the Power within you. Nothing can stay your upward climb, there is nobody who can prevent you succeeding except yourself; there is nothing that can stop your progress but your own doubt and fear. All things are possible if you believe that they are possible.

Unbounded confidence, the keynote of Success. YOU cannot fail, YOU, yourself, are Success.

Another word for "unbounded confidence" is "faith." Every successful man is a confident man. He believes wholeheartedly in his own power to succeed. This is not vanity or being too "cock-sure," instead it is either conscious, or unconscious, or sub-conscious realization of the Inward Power. This is why so few men are really successful, so few men ever arouse the mighty powers that are within them, so few men think the kind of thoughts that bring these powers into life and action.

Every successful man is a man of "faith," every successful man is a man who cultivates "hope." A successful man is always hopeful, is never a pessimist and he brings that which he hopes for, into being and reality, by the strength of his faith.

Therefore I want you first of all to cultivate Hope and Faith for without those qualities no one, no matter how gifted or clever, can ever succeed.

That you have these two qualities is proved by the fact that you are reading this course. You have had the hope of winning your way to a life of Success, and Power, and you have had the Faith to believe that within you are the powers and forces which make this possible. Without Hope a man is as good as dead, without Faith he is like a rudderless ship drifting hither and thither with every wind and current. On the other hand all things are possible to the man who has both these qualities.

Cast your eyes over the lives of all men of great achievement, and you will see that they were all animated by Hope and sustained by Faith. They hoped for success and believed that they had it in them to achieve that success. In their darkest hours they hoped on, believing that soon the reaction would come, which would carry them on to the accomplishment of their ambitions. Nothing has ever yet been accomplished by man on this planet without the inspiration of Hope and the tenacity of Faith. Hope reaches forward and claims success, faith holds on until success is attained. Therefore seek to develop these qualities to their fullest extent.

It is a well known fact that when a man turns his face round and determines to fight his way to success, or to overcome evil habit, or to raise himself in any way either mentally, morally, physically or spiritually, then everything seems to happen to thwart his new intention and to throttle his new desires. So long as he goes on in his old way, drifting with the tide, floating about helplessly, the sport of fate and the prey of outside circumstances, so long as this goes on, nothing unusual happens. But directly a start is made in an upward direction, then all kinds of psychic powers seem to be let loose, whose object appears to be to prevent the student from making any progress in his new life.

When a man realizes his own interior powers and understands the vastness and wonder of his subliminal forces, and determines to make use of them, and thus become a king among men instead of a slave, then such a disturbance takes place that unless he possesses Hope and Faith he will be tempted to turn his back on the new life and to sink back again into the old sluggish drifting existence, which leads to disappointment and despair.

Those people variously known as Christian Scientists, Mental Scientists, Spiritual Scientists, etc. (no matter what they call themselves, they all deal with the powers of the mind) all experience the same thing. Even the health is affected in a curious way, friends are peevish and irritable, little things go wrong in business, and generally one is out of sorts and all things awry.

When this experience comes to one, then is the time to exercise Hope and Faith. First of all remember that the condition is only temporary. After a few days, in some cases it may be weeks, the health will improve, friends will become genial and harmony will again reign in your life. When the entities that cause the disturbance realize that you mean to keep on, and that you cannot be bullied into going back to the old life, they will quickly leave you. In any case there is nothing to be afraid of, because these entities are helpless if one does not fear them. In other words, if you have Hope and Faith you can win through. Hope for better times although the present may be discouraging. Faith in the sure belief that soon all the disagreeable symptoms will disappear. Hope on; by Faith, hang on, and keep hanging on and you will win through. Do not be discouraged by seeming failure, nothing was ever won without effort. What can be had without effort is not worth having.

Take encouragement from the fact that this disturbance in your life proves that vital changes are taking place within, that the vast powers of your subliminal mind are beginning to awaken, and that the entities of your old erroneous beliefs and habits are taking their departure.

Believe now that you can conquer and win through, and you will conquer and win through. What you believe you can do, you can do, because all power is within you. There is nothing in all the world that can stop you, except your own doubt and fear.

I want you to trust me to the extent of doing something, the underlying principle of which cannot be explained in this first lesson. I want you to make what is known as an "affirmation," I want you to affirm the following: "THE OLD LIFE IS DEAD AND BURIED. I HAVE SEVERED MYSELF FROM IT ONCE AND FOR ALL. HENCEFORTH I LIVE THE NEW LIFE OF SUCCESS AND POWER, OF SELF-MASTERY AND ALL ACCOMPLISHMENT."

First of all memorize these words. Keep repeating them over until they sink deeply into your memory, and their meaning finds a place in your consciousness. If you can get a few moments to yourself during the day, practice making the affirmations. The right way is as follows: Go into a quiet place, whether you sit, stand, or lie down is immaterial. Now close your eyes and say the words over very earnestly.

Strive to realize all that they mean and address the words to your inner mind. It is your submerged mind that you are influencing, so address the affirmation very earnestly to it. Do this for several minutes, and finish by making the affirmation into space. Hurl it out as a message to the Universe and by so doing you will come into harmony with innumerable invisible forces, who will help and strengthen you. Do not make the affirmation while in a state of strain and nervous tension. Relax yourself, take a deep breath, and as you exhale let your muscles go limp; smooth out your nerves until your whole body is in a peaceful easy state. Concentrate your thoughts on what you are doing. If they wander bring them back and begin again. The more you concentrate the better will be the result.

The most important, in fact the time above all times for making the affirmation is just as you are falling to sleep. There is a great psychological reason for this. If you can fall asleep while making the affirmation, or while visualizing it, so much the better. Therefore take no food or stimulants (it is better to avoid the latter altogether) just before retiring. The reason cannot be given here because it would take too long, but it is an important one.

In the early morning immediately on waking is the next best time, both times should be made use of, and on no account be missed, but of the two the one just before sleep is by far the more important. The influence of these two affirmations will be felt during the day, they will have an effect upon your mental outlook, and upon the way in which you will deal with the problems of your day's work; but this influence can be intensified and buttressed up, as it were, by "retiring into yourself" at intervals, during the day, and mentally repeating the affirmation. This will give you a sense of power and confidence and hope, such as you have never experienced before. This is not "imagination," it is your hitherto unsuspected interior powers being aroused into activity.

When you have finished making the affirmation, again close your eyes and make a mental picture of yourself in the manner already taught. Endeavor to see yourself a radiant being, with the old life and its murkiness and imperfections left far behind you. Picture yourself pressing forward to higher and better things, meeting difficulties, it is true, but overcoming them, trampling old habits, weaknesses and imperfections under your feet. Try and realize that you have the power to raise yourself above the ordinary things of life, that you can breathe a rarer and purer atmosphere. Picture yourself as a new being, happier, healthier, brighter and more radiant than ever you have been even at your most sublime moments.

This will not be easy. It requires concentration and perseverance. You will find it difficult to see yourself as you wish to see yourself, or you will find it not easy to see yourself clearly at all, also you will find it difficult to keep your mind concentrated upon the making of the image. There is only one thing to do and that is to keep on trying. Thus in the first lesson do you come face to face with a battle royal. With most students this visualizing is a great difficulty, but no matter how difficult it may be, it has to be overcome. If you fail to overcome this difficulty then you fail in this course of lessons; if you fail to overcome now, you will fail in the larger things of life.

The best way to overcome a difficulty is by getting interested in it. When you have developed interest, enthusiasm is aroused, and after that concentration becomes comparatively easy, and this commands success. Therefore get interested in this problem of visualizing. Remember that all men of great achievement have had this power greatly developed, therefore if you wish to be great and successful you must first develop this same faculty.

There has never been a great act or achievement in the world's history that was not first visualized in this manner. Everything is first created in the unseen before it is manifested in the seen. When you, by dint of practice, can visualize clearly and distinctly, you will have developed creative power, not figuratively, but literally so.

Whatever you create in your mental world by means of visualizing will in time be manifested in the outer physical world. The outer world of matter is subservient to the inner world of mind. This is a great occult truth which has been withheld from ordinary people and has been until recently the closely guarded secret of certain secret orders. It is now given into your hands, you are put upon your honor not to reveal it to others. When they have reached a certain stage of their development, the knowledge will come to them by some channel or other, and in the meantime it does more harm than good to try to impart occult knowledge to those who are not interested or ready to receive it.

I hope enough has been said to arouse your interest in, and enthusiasm for, visualizing. The more clearly you can visualize, the more clean cut will be the results in your daily life. This creative power can be so highly developed that a sick man can make himself well, a poor man can change his circumstances from poverty to prosperity, and a miserable and despondent pessimist can change himself into a cheery, optimist. By visualizing, and by denials and affirmations (which will be explained later), by meditation and by the exercise of Hope and Faith the life, character and circumstances can be transformed. The results are so extraordinary that it is very difficult to get people to believe them, but they are none the less real. Therefore practice your affirmations and persevere with your visualizing, they will lead to results of which you can at present form but a faint conception.

To obtain the best results from this course it is necessary to set apart a special time every day for meditation and concentration. The reason man is so weak and unhappy is because he lives the whole of his time in the objective life, the shallow material life of the senses, and neglects the deeper, grander and transcendental life of the inner mind. It is the inner life that gives power and peace and satisfaction. The outer material life of the infinite mind of the senses only bring worry and care, the inner life of the deeper mind brings strength, wisdom, understanding and ability to accomplish and achieve.

It is a proved scientific fact that you grow into the likeness of that upon which you meditate. If you meditate upon evil then evil will come into your life; if you meditate upon revenge, your life will be turned into an inferno of trouble; on the other hand, if you meditate upon happiness and other higher mental states, then happiness will be yours, and if you let your thoughts dwell upon "peace" then peace of mind will result. All these states and many others are within you; they can be called forth by meditation. You can call forth either good or evil, success or failure, strength or weakness, happiness or woe, everything is in your own hands.

MEDITATION I

To be used every day and twice a day if possible, between the hours of 6 and 9 a.m. and 9 and 11:30 p.m. Other times are suitable, but those mentioned will be found especially valuable to students, as between these hours their teacher is meditating upon the same thoughts, and the vibrations from his mind will be helpful to all who are "tuned to receive them."

Try and arrange to spend half an hour in meditation before retiring for the night. Sit in a quiet place, relax your body and concentrate upon these words:

Within me are infinite powers seeking expression. In the past, because I did not know of their existence, they have been stifled and suppressed. Now I "will" that they shall be called into activity, and find perfect and full expression in my body in the form of perfect health, in my life in the form of success and achievement, in my heart in the form of a mighty upwelling of joy and happiness. Now that I have discovered this hidden and inexhaustible store of power and energy, my life is transformed; weakness gives place to strength, sorrow to happiness, morbidness to radiant joy, pessimism to divine optimism, despair to hope, failure to success, poverty to prosperity, sickness to health. Henceforth only the highest good can come into my life. Now by the power of my thought-forces I am allied with and joined to the Infinite Principle of Good, and we have become one. Henceforth for me there is, and can be, no evil, only Infinite Good. All evil is now cast out of my life, because I am one with the Infinite Good. "No evil can come nigh my dwelling"; "nothing can harm or destroy." Henceforth by scientific thinking I control my life, for my life is the result or effect of my thoughts. When evil thoughts, or weak thoughts, or impure thoughts, or failure thoughts, or fear thoughts, or poverty thoughts, or hate thoughts, or disease thoughts assail me, I will cast them out and think only of thoughts of love, and strength, of health and prosperity, of success and achievement, and of the Infinite Perfection with which I am now allied, and of which I form a part.

When meditating upon the above, take each thought separately in turn and concentrate all your thoughts upon it. Not only grasp its meaning, but try and picture what it means. For instance: "My life is transformed." When you think upon these words, try and see your life being transformed, see your weaknesses falling away from you like an old garment, and instead, strength, success and noble qualities being born in their place. Practice and concentrate and FEEL the power of this meditation.

This ends the metaphysical part of this week's lesson, the following are some brief hints of great value to the student beginning the study of Scientific Thought: (1) Everything works according to Law, we each of us have what we deserve. (2) Covet no man's goods, possessions or happiness; he deserves them, let him alone. Realize that the Universe holds all that you can possibly desire--for you. (3) Hate no man. Hatred will come back like a boomerang and hurt you far more than it can the object of your hatred. Ignore what you cannot like, and concentrate your mind on pleasant things. (4) Be true, be honest, be faithful. All these create vibrations which will bring back blessings and happiness to you.

You have entered a life, the power and possibilities of which you at present have no conception. If I described it now you would not understand. But, believe me, it is a life of Power to accomplish and Victory over all weaknesses. It is a life of Prosperity and true Success. It is a life of transcendent Joy. It is a life of peace and blessing to your fellows.

Look up. Keep looking up. Keep on affirming. Keep on visualizing. Keep on meditating. Keep on believing. Keep on hoping. What you hope for, and believe, and affirm, and visualize, is yours. Remember also that you grow into the likeness of that which you meditate upon. The brain is a very delicate instrument; it is the vehicle through which the mind finds expression. The mind cannot manifest its power if the brain is clouded by grossness of body. The one who would improve his or her mind, who would awaken the mighty powers within, must give up hurtful physical habits. It is useless to attempt to eradicate bad mental habits while the body is suffering from indulgence of any kind. For instance, it would be waste of time to affirm all or any of the higher qualities of the mind and then to go to bed intoxicated or full of pork chops and fried onions. Let your diet be on the light side, always rise from the table slightly hungry rather than repleted, and never eat later than three hours before retiring to bed. For instance, if you go to bed at 11 p. m. do not eat at a later hour than 8 p. m. This is a most important point, the affirmations have more power if made when fasting, therefore the last thing at night and the time of waking in the early morning are the best times at which to perform them. There are physical and psychological reasons for this. Bathe the body every day and follow by rough towelling. Do not wear too much clothing. Avoid tight collars and neck bands.

Take a fair amount of exercise, walking is the best form for most people. When walking keep the shoulders fairly well back, the back hollow and the body well balanced over the hips. Above all keep the head up. Do not look down, but LOOK UP. There is a reason for this.

As regards diet, eat the food that agrees with you best, but eat if you can digest them one or two raw things every day; raw ripe fruit, salad, water cress, etc.; again there is a reason. Masticate each mouthful of food until it becomes liquid.

Get into the habit of breathing deeply and through the nose. Keep the mouth firmly closed. Keep your windows open night and day, fresh air is cheap.

Lastly, try always to maintain a cheerful frame of mind.

APPENDIX

It will be helpful for you to think of your subliminal Mind as another person, one who is always listening, listening, listening. He hears all that you say, and ACTS UPON all the thoughts that you let pass the threshold of the inner mind.

"Hush! he is listening," should be the watch-word of your life. Let no thought of evil, of impurity, of weakness, of ill-health, of failure, of hate, of anger, of fear, enter your Subliminal Mind, for he will receive them as orders which he will obey, and being all-powerful, great and terrible will be the results. Therefore let only thoughts of good, purity, strength, health, success, love, self-control, courage and determination enter this greater mind of vast intelligence and power. Do this, and your Subliminal Mind will take these thoughts as orders, and will shape your life and health accordingly. Thus in a general way your Subliminal Mind will be led to develop your life on healthful and successful, noble and harmonious lines.

The visualizing taught in this course, also the denials (explained later), affirmations, meditations and other exercises, all have a very strong, deep, scientific purpose in view, and this is the training of the Subliminal Mind. The Affirmation and the Visualizing taught in this lesson are given you in order to make a definite impression upon your Subliminal Mind.

The main object of this lesson is to make a dent or impression on the Subliminal Mind and to make it realize that the old life is dead and that you have now entered a new life of health, success and power. Your Subliminal Mind will accept this if you persevere with the visualizing and affirmations, and will thus be prepared for the more advanced training which is to follow.

Let "Hush! he is listening" be the watch-word of your life.

PART II

GAZE up into the sky at night and sense the infinite majesty of the Universe. Get mentally into touch with those patient stars that flash and twinkle like gems of purest water. Realize that they are suns, situated millions of miles away. Then think of our own little spot in the Universe--the Solar System. Think of the majestic Magnetic Sun; the planets all following certain paths guided by a wonderful system of Universal Law. Observe the precision of the rising and setting of the Sun, the lunar periods, the rhythmic ebb and flow of the tidal sea. Let your mind grasp what all this means, let it sweep right from the grandest aspect of Nature down to the atom itself and what does it see? A Power expressing itself in an infinite variety of ways, in everything, and through everything. There is nothing, not a grain, not an atom, not an electron, that does not contain this wondrous Power. Man has been described as an epitome of the Universe; an atom clairvoyantly observed has been described as a replica of the Solar System; therefore we have universe within universe, solar system within solar system, and all animated, controlled and directed by the Universal or Infinite Mind.

Therefore the Power that animates man is an Infinite Power--in man the Infinite Mind finds its highest expression on the visible plane.

At one time man was thought to be an animal with a soul. Now he is known to be an indestructible Ego with an imperishable Mind finding expression in a temporary physical body. The cause of all man's weakness, mistakes and failures, has been that he has not realized the Power within; instead, he has thought himself to be separate and friendless, weak and helpless, adrift, without chart or compass upon the sea of life. He has thought himself to be the victim of circumstance, the sport of fate, and the puppet of forces outside himself. He has called himself a worm instead of looking upon himself as a king. He has though, himself to be worthless and insignificant instead of realizing his wonderful interior. POWERS and the grandeur of his being.

Instead of being a worm, man is a king. Potentially all the powers of the Infinite Mind are his. Instead of being the victim of circumstances he can control them. Instead of being the puppet of forces outside himself, he has within him the Power to be what he will; to do what he will; to accomplish all that he desires.

Now at last the darkness is being pierced and man realizes that he is a mental creature, and that he is MIND as well as matter, that is, as Mind, is one with the Universal or Infinite MIND. That the difference between him and the Infinite or Universal MIND is not one of kind, but of degree.

Like a traveller lost in the bush, who, almost dying, at last finds his way to a permanent spring of water, and drinks and drinks again, knowing that he can never exhaust the everlasting supply; so does man after long wanderings, at last realize, that within him is a fountain of never failing Power and Wisdom, and that his subliminal mind is linked up with, and forms a part of, the Infinite Mind of the Universe.

This is the greatest discovery in the history of the World; this is the crowning revelation of all the ages; this is the blinding knowledge that dwarfs every other knowledge THAT WITHIN MAN DWELLS THE INFINITE AND UNFATHOMABLE MIND OF THE UNIVERSE.

Call how he may on these hidden forces, they can never fail to respond, for they are infinite and inexhaustible. Man stands alone and apart from all other creatures, in this visible world around him, in that he has the power to govern his own actions, choose right or wrong, to mould his own fate, and create his own life and circumstances.

To other creatures, life and the visible world are fixed quantities. To man, life and the world are reflexes of inward mental states. Thus, can he make life what he will; thus can he live in a world of his own creating.

Man alone has the power to realize and recognize the inward Power of the Infinite, and to consciously bring It into objectivity.

The inward powers of the mind are potentially illimitable, but they lie dormant and unexpressed, until they are recognized, and aroused into action, by the individual.

This is why the majority of people are so worried and distressed. Why they either fail to make life worth living or achieve only partial success, and that with great difficulty. They try to achieve without the power to achieve. They marvel at their own weakness, not realizing that within them lie immeasurable powers which are patiently waiting to find expression.

Until man calls these powers into activity they can never act. Within him is that which is connected with the Power-House of the Universe, yet he never feels its power. Within him is Infinite Wisdom, Knowledge, Inspiration, Creative Power and driving Force, yet he slumbers on, unconscious of their existence. But to those who realize their own interior Powers. what a mine of inexhaustible treasure do they find, what force and energy for all accomplishment

When you, dear reader, enter into the realization of the mighty Power within you, you enter into possession of all good and perfect things. You cease to strive, and squabble, and snatch, with selfish anxious hand, the bread from another's mouth. You leave off striving, with palpitating heart and careworn face, to push your way in front of the one next to you. Instead, you set your ambitions high, and sustained and carried forward by invisible forces, enter into possession of all that you desire. Work? Yes, you will work, for right thinking--and this realization of the Power within you is the result of right thinking--is the inspiration of all right action. You will work hard enough--and no one is happy who does not work--but the difference will be that your work will be the greatest joy in your joyful life. Joy! there is no joy like the joy of work well loved and well done, and which leads to accomplishment and victory. Work! yes, you will work, but not with the feverish haste or with the fear of failure and bankruptcy ever before you. Instead, you will work with confidence and power, sure in the knowledge, that your efforts lead definitely to Success.

When you have realized the inward Power, you will feel it pushing you in the back and impelling you forward, you will feel yourself borne along to the goal of your endeavor.

Whereas formerly you were chasing Success, and waiting on it cap in hand; in future you will realize that you are master; that you command and Success obeys. You realize that instead of as in the past, running after fame and fortune, which, like a will o' the wisp, constantly eluded you, you have now the power to attract all desirable things to you.

Instead of feverish anxiety and joyless quest, you possess calm confidence and the power to accomplish everything that you desire.

There will be no anxiety, no care for the morrow; instead--the confidence of exact knowledge--the knowledge that the results will be exactly as arranged. Just as today is the result of past thinking, so the future will be the result of what is built today. Therefore you do certain things today and you KNOW with mathematical certainty what the future results will be.

Like John Burroughs you can say:

"I stay my haste, I make delays,
For what avails this anxious pace,
I stand amid eternal ways,
And what is mine shall know my face."

"What is mine shall know my face," that is the basis of all success, the confidence, the exact knowledge that what you are sowing now will be reaped a hundredfold; that in the future you will enter into occupation of that which you are building now, that what you claim as your own NOW, out of all the riches of the Universal Store House, will be yours in the future. It is yours NOW, you enter into possession in the days to come.

You will now begin to see why I ask you to use affirmations. In succeeding lessons will be explained what affirmations are, their object and the manner in which they work.

In the meantime make use of the same affirmation that you have been using in the past week, but with something added. It will now read: The old life is dead and buried. I have severed myself from it once and for all. Henceforth I live the new life of Success and Power, Self-Mastery and all Accomplishment. This I do, not in the strength of my feeble will and surface mind of my ordinary consciousness, but by the Infinite Power of my deeper inner MIND which is one with, and forms a part of, the Infinite Universal Mind.

Make the affirmations earnestly. Think of what you are saying. Enter into all that the words mean. Try and feel their power. Do not, however, screw yourself up to a nervous tension, instead let yourself relax. First your body with its muscles and nerves--let them all go limp, then your mind--let that unbend also. Now affirm calmly and confidently as instructed, and then visualize a picture of yourself, radiant, calm, and possessed of a new power. See yourself master of all weaknesses and passions, directing yourself, guiding your life with unerring wisdom, shaping your course to a glorious destiny. Practice and keep on practicing the art of visualizing. Remember that you are dealing with finer matter than that which is discerned by the senses, but it is none the less real; in fact, it is far more real. The fact that you can see with your mind's eye that which you have created by your mental processes, is proof that what you have created exists. If it did not exist you could not see it, If, therefore, you create in your mental realm a picture of yourself, radiant, successful, self disciplined, master of your life and destiny, then you are creating a new YOU which in process of time will become objectified in your outward life. In other words, the new YOU, the radiant being of your mental imagery, will later manifest itself in a new outside physical YOU. Whatever is created in the Unseen, later becomes manifested in the Seen. This is an immutable Law. By mental imagery you create in the Unseen. Be careful what you create, whatever it is, good or bad, will find its way into your life and be read and known of all men.

Whenever you meet with temptation or difficulty or if you let yourself get flustered at business, just "retire into yourself" tor a moment and make the affirmation mentally, and "realize" that you are a new creature. You will then become conscious of THE INWARD POWER.

MEDITATION NO. 2

Sit very quietly and relax nerves and muscles, and concentrate your thoughts upon a conception of an ideal world. Picture a world of indescribable beauty, without pain, sickness or care; without hate, unkindness or selfishness; without poverty, want or any lack. Picture mentally a world in which love and good will reign supreme, where beauty, joy, happiness, plenty and profusion of all good things are unstinted and for all. Picture a world where there is no limitation, where you can know everything, possess all the wisdom, and where you can be everywhere at the same time.

In this world the colors of the flowers and of the sky are more beautiful and transparent than anything you have seen before, the singing of the birds more ravishing than anything yet heard. The inhabitants are all comely and gloriously healthy and strong, they are all animated by good will and indescribably happy. This is the perfect World of MIND.

Now concentrate upon this image. You will most probably find worry thoughts intruding. Thoughts of the rent, of the mistake one of your clerks has made in your business, of threatened competition, or of some slander or unkind imputation that may have been made against you. Whenever a thought tries to enter your mind dismiss it at once and concentrate your mind upon your ideal world. This will not be easy, but continue to persevere. It is most important that you should master this, as by so doing you are cultivating one of the most wonderful faculties of your mind. Therefore keep on dismissing the unwelcome thought by denying it. For instance, you are disturbed by the thought that something grossly unfair has been done to you, it makes your blood boil when you think of it. Immediately this thought comes to you, say at once, "in this perfect world of Mind there is no unfairness, in justice or unkindness, all is truth and honor and good will," and raise your thoughts above this imperfect material life, and concentrate your mental gaze upon your ideal world. Again, a thought may come suggesting that the new competition in your business will ruin you. Immediately deny it by saying, "in this perfect world there is no competition, there is no failure; I am a perfect mental creature gifted with Infinite Powers, and I am above competition, I am success." Keep your mental vision on your ideal world the whole time and keep denying all your troubles one by one, and affirming their opposites.

By your denials you "kill" the worry thought and by affirming its opposite you build up a character and mental outlook that are superior to worry and incapable of failure.

NOT ONLY DO YOU KILL THE THOUGHT OF EVIL, YOU ALSO DESTROY THE EVIL ITSELF.

This may sound fantastic to you, but E. is ABSOLUTELY TRUE. Later on you will be able to PROVE the truth of this beyond the shadow of a doubt.

APPENDIX

It was seen in last week's Appendix that in a general way the Subliminal Mind could be influenced for good by allowing only thoughts of good, courage, health, success, etc., to pass the citadel of the mind. This is the foundation of all happiness and harmony in one's life, but if it is desired to arouse your latent powers, and to train your Subliminal to solve all your problems, to give you true inspiration and supply you with original ideas, other methods must be employed. Your great Subliminal Mind is not going to yield up its wonderful store of knowledge, neither is it going to act as the solver of all your problems, in response to a mere pious wish. What is necessary is, that very strong, concentrated, forceful directed thoughts should be sent down into this greater mind, continuously and persistently. Whatever message you keep sending down into your Subliminal Mind, provided it is not changed or altered, and that it is sufficiently strong and concentrated, will be obeyed--in time. Some students will be longer than others, but every one sooner or later, who follows these instructions, will develop the power of directed Subliminal thinking.

The first step is to impress very powerfully upon the Subliminal Mind that it is capable of solving all your problems. At present unless you are a very rare exception, your Subliminal Mind is hypnotized into the belief that it cannot solve your problems. So long as it believes that it cannot solve your problems it never will attempt the task, but once you can convince your Subliminal Mind that it has the power, the wisdom and knowledge to do so, then you will at once pass from weakness to power. You will have at your disposal a mind so vast and wonderful that the finite mind of the senses will be unable to grasp its full significance.

In order to convince your Subliminal Mind that it can solve all your problems you must (1) believe yourself that it can do so, (2) have a strong desire to use your hidden powers, (3) make strong affirmations that your Subliminal Mind can think constructively and drawing upon the All-knowledge solve every perplexity and problem, and (4) visualize yourself meeting with problems and having them solved immediately by referring them to your greater mind within.

Within you are limitless powers, but they only become available when you consciously call upon them and make use of them. Therefore carry this thought strongly in your mind, "My Subliminal Mind can draw upon the Universal Intelligence and solve all my problems."

When seeking to impress the Subliminal Mind it is necessary to get alone and to still the objective mind and the senses. When all thoughts of worry, business and material life, have been dismissed from the mind and perfect mental calm obtained, then you will be in a state favorable to (1) the sending of directions to the Subliminal Mind, and (2) receiving inspiration from it.

HEALTH

We have seen in this lesson that within man dwells the Universal Mind, and that when he looks within he finds infinite power. In the same way man is also animated by the Infinite Life. So long as man ignores the infinite nature of his life, so long will he be weak, diseased, ill and miserable. The animal health of our fathers is passing away, and man is becoming more sensitive, more mental, more spiritual, and therefore depends more and more upon mental and spiritual forces for his life and health. Everyone is getting more nervous and highly strung, more imaginative, more sensitive to the power of thought and other spiritual and psychic forces. Therefore, man must look more and more to the one Source of all Life for his health, energy and vitality.

Those who seek perfect health, and who does not these days, should deny every thought of and belief in sickness, illness and disease and constantly affirm and visualize a state of perfect health and well-being. Always before your mental vision let this idea of health be dominant, let it be a pillar of cloud by day and a pillar of fire by night, leading you ever out of the land of bondage and sickness into the promised land of perfect radiant health.

The Unseen is greater than the Seen, therefore to work in the Unseen is to deal with the "cause" of which the outward life is the "effect." By working in the Unseen by means of meditation, affirmation, visualizing and by holding in our mind the highest ideals we arouse the Power that lies hidden within us.

The Power that is within us is the power of the Universal Mind or Spirit, therefore it is infinite and illimitable; the only limit there can be is the limitation we place upon it by our lack of faith.

Therefore in all your difficulties and battles remember that the Power within you is infinite. You are one with the Infinite if you will only believe it, if you can only realize it.

Rise up and go forward with confidence, your highest ideals can. be attained too, if you will believe and have faith and reach upward to higher and better things.

I affirm for you the inward knowledge of these things.

PART III

WHILE the existence of the subliminal mind is a modern discovery to Western minds, it is ancient knowledge in the East. For centuries this knowledge has been treasured by certain orders of mystics. Dating right back to the earliest times we find evidence of signs and wonders being worked through the power of the subliminal mind.

In the West, however, there has always been a tendency toward materialism. A materialist believes in matter. He wants to see, touch and handle before he will believe.

Literally he will only believe what he sees through the senses, Modern science has, however, knocked the ground from under the materialist's feet, because it is constantly proving that there is far more in the unseen than there is in the seen. Science, in spite of all its achievements, realizes that, up to the present, it has only been paddling on the edge of a mighty ocean of mystery.

Science has, slowly and with huge and clumsy effort, now proved the existence of many things which scientists would not believe before, but which were known to the ancients, and have been known in the East for centuries. One of these is the existence of the subliminal mind. Mesmerism and Hypnotism have proved that man is composed of more than one MIND. There is the surface or outside mind of the senses. This mind reasons, learns from books and other outside sources, and function generally, on the physical plane. It is only a minute fraction of the total mind of man. Like the iceberg which only shows one-twelfth of itself above the surface of the sea, the other eleven-twelfths being submerged, the objective mind of man is only an infinitesimal portion of the whole. The surface or objective mind is the finite mind, the Subliminal is joined up with the Universal Mind of the Universe, therefore it can never be measured, it is beyond comprehension. Sufficient for us to know that its power is limitless, and that we can use this power in creating our lives anew, and for the realization of all our desires.

The Subliminal Mind is (1) inspiratory, (2) intuitive, and (3) creative. It is a store-house of knowledge and the power-house of energy. It is much more than all this, how much no one knows. In this lesson we will consider the first three descriptions in the order named.

(1) Inspiration. It is through the subliminal mind that all inspiration has come to men. It was through this channel that Wordsworth, Shakespeare, Milton, Emerson and all great teachers, preachers and leaders have drawn their inspiration. All the good that has ever come into this world has been through inspiration; and all inspiration comes through the subliminal mind.

All who have ever accomplished anything worth accomplishing have done so through the inspiration of their subliminal mind. That some are giants in their accomplishments and others pigmies is simply due to differing degrees of expression. Some express more of the Power within them, some express less. The Power is there, it is for us to express it. We cannot all be Shakespeares and Miltons, neither is it possible for all men to be Gladstones or Lincolns, but there is a niche somewhere in the world where we can each find a useful field of congenial work. We can, if we will, be guided by inspiration, find somewhere a field of labor where we can pour out our pent up passion for achievement, where we can command success beyond our wildest dreams.

You, dear reader, have not been sent into this world for a joke, you have been sent to achieve a certain purpose, to accomplish something which no one can do but you. There is no one in all the world just like you, and all that you do is colored by your individuality. No one in all the world could do your work just as you do it; there are fields of conquest in front of you which no one out you can conquer. Therefore listen to the voice of inspiration.

(2) Intuitive. Those who learn to recognize the voice of intuition are brought into touch with infinite wisdom. They do by intuition that which other people can only do by cumbersome effort, if indeed they can do it at all. One who has developed this power has no perplexities, because all his problems are solved for him by his subliminal mind. He listens to the inner voice of wisdom, acts accordingly, and the result always justifies his faith in this inward power.

President Lincoln, when confronted by a perplexing problem. used to make a habit of dismissing it to his inner mind; and then going for a short walk. During his walk he would interest himself in the birds and trees and other things around him and then give no thought to the perplexity which was demanding an answer. When he got back from his walk the answer would be ready--his subliminal mind had solved the problem. Others, puzzled by an intricate matter, may go to bed with the problem still unsolved, and awake in the morning with the solution of their difficulty already formed in their conscious mind; or it may come to them, like a flash, while they are dressing; the subliminal mind has solved their problem.

In the subliminal mind is all wisdom and understanding. You, too, can use this wisdom and understanding if you develop the faculty of inward hearing.

(3) Creative. The subliminal mind is creative. Being one with the Universal Mind, which is the Creative Power of the Universe, it partakes of the same nature. The difference is not one of kind but of degree.

As in the macrocosm, so in the microcosm. Just as Infinite Mind is absolute through the whole Universe, so is man king of his life, master of his fate, captain of his soul, creator of his life and circumstances.

Man cannot create a planet, but he can consciously form an image or picture in his creative mind, a picture of better circumstance, different environment or definite achievement, and holding that image persistently compel it to materialize in his life and circumstances. This is not a fairy tale--it is a hard, common sense fact. There is nothing that has ever been accomplished by man that has not first been created and imaged in his mind. It is always the vision first, and afterwards the accomplishment. The difference between men is a difference of vision. The difference between their vision is the difference between their accomplishment. Some men create more than others--it is because theirs is a greater vision. All the great ones of the earth, leaders of men and nations, artists, poets, inventors, financiers, have been what they were because of their "vision," because they were men of "imagination."

People who pride themselves on being "practical" look askance at imagination, thinking it to be something impractical and shadowy; something belonging to the realm of dreams. They confuse constructive imagery with day dreaming. Now, the imagination of which I am speaking is the very antithesis of day dreaming. Day dreaming is the aimless frittering away of the mental powers; creative imagination, on the other hand, gathers together the mental forces, and by focusing the powers of the hidden mind bring into being a definite image. This definite image is the vision which all men of accomplishment possess.

This vision is the basis of all achievement. It is impossible to name a single great man or woman who has not been inspired and guided by it. The reason that here and there in the world's history there have been great characters who have achieved the noblest ends is because theirs have been the noblest visions. It is impossible to create a poor, puny, low kind of image in the mind, and then to win great success in life. As the image is, so your life will be. Therefore if you hold in your mind the vision, or mental picture, of great success or noble endeavor, then in your life these things will become manifested. It cannot be otherwise--because what is held in the mind is later manifested in the life.

Thus it is that a person of poor powers of concentration cannot hold a definite image in his mind, but must be always changing and modifying it, with the result that he gets nothing but confusion and lack of achievement manifested in his life. What you are inwardly, what you think inwardly, what you visualize inwardly, is what your future life will be. Your outward life is modeled on your inward life--it is an exact replica of the life within.

Therefore your subliminal mind is not only the source of inspiration and intuition, it is creative also. Your life is in your own hands, you can make it what you will. Your future is yours entirely, you can build it up with mathematical precision into any form you please. You are free to make or to mar, to build up or destroy. You can climb to the highest heights or descend to the lowest depths. You can be weak or strong, filthy or pure, miserable or happy, unsuccessful or successful, poverty stricken or prosperous, ill or healthy, hated or loved: It is all a matter of Thought-control and Scientific Thinking.

It is now time that you begin to apply some of the things you have learned. Therefore add to your affirmation at night the following:

MINE IS A LIFE OF OVERCOMING AND POWER.

Henceforward I will cease doing ...... and will instead do ......

I do this by the Infinite Power within me which can never fail.

Where I have left blanks I want you to fill in with (1) whatever bad habit you most wish to eradicate, and (2) to insert the virtue which you wish to put in its place. For instance suppose you have been in the habit of getting up late, swallowing your breakfast hurriedly and rushing to business, getting all behind with appointments and correspondence, developing indigestion, headache and peevishness in consequence. Supposing this is the case (of course I only use this as an illustration), you will fill in the words to suit, so that the sentence will read something like this, supposing your proper time for rising to be 7 a. m.:

Henceforward I will cease getting up late and will instead get up punctually at 7 a. m

or better still, you can command yourself to wake at 6:30 and spend half an hour in meditations and the saying of affirmations, You will then be quite ready to rise at 7 o'clock.

Immediately following the affirmation, visualize a picture of yourself waking in the morning. "See" yourself open your eyes and look at the clock. "See" that the time is 6:30. "See" yourself engaged in concentration, meditation and making of affirmations. "See" yourself look at the clock again, and at 7 o'clock "see" yourself get up and go to the bath room. The more clearly you can picture this scene the easier will you find the task of getting up to be.

You may not be successful the first morning or two, but if you persevere you will find that you have by the use of affirmations complete control over yourself. The more successful you become the stronger does your Will-power grow.

If you are in the habit of going to bed too late you can add to your morning affirmation the following:

"Henceforward I will cease going to bed late. I will instead go to bed at 10. At 10 o'clock tonight I shall feel sleepy and tired. I will then go to bed."

After making this affirmation, visualize yourself as you will appear at 10 p. m. You are, we will say, sitting reading or working. You "see" yourself look at the clock. You "see" yourself put your book or work away and go to bed. Persevere with the visualizing until you can see every detail with great vividness and distinctness.

Make this affirmation and create this mental picture and you will find that what you have affirmed and visualized will come to pass exactly as desired. Before you is unfolding a life of perfect self-control and overcoming. When you have become master of yourself, first in small things and then in the greater, you will have become master over your life, your circumstances and your destiny.

Not only is it necessary that you should overcome habits in this way by reversing them, but it is also necessary that you should reverse all your wrong ideas of life and the Universe, replacing wrong and harmful ideas by Truth. One of the objects of this course is to dispel old erroneous beliefs, and thus to change your mental outlook. In addition it is necessary that you should reverse every thought and suggestion of a harmful character directly it comes to you. A thought may come to you such as: "You will fail, you can never succeed." Now if you allow that thought to enter your mind it will weaken you, paralyze your efforts and bring failure into your life, just as surely as day follows night. Therefore as soon as it comes to you you must kill it by denial. In this case you would raise yourself in thought to your perfect mental world and say, "There is no failure. I am a perfect Mental creature living in a perfect Mental World, all the potentialities of the Infinite Mind are mine. I cannot fail." Say this over several times and then affirm: "I am Success, within me are Infinite Powers; I am success in all that I undertake."

Every time that you do this you drive failure further and further away and establish success more firmly in your life. The oftener you do this, provided that you get a clear concept of your perfect Mental World, and, as it were, breathe its atmosphere. the more rapidly you will progress. Do not, however, strain and worry after results, instead seek to adopt and maintain a calm, serene, confident attitude, above the worries and cares of life.

Again, the thought may come to you, "there is that pain again, I am going to have one of my bad attacks." If you allow this thought to enter your mind you will have that bad "attack"; it will surely come and nothing will be able to keep it away. The "attack" is only effect, the cause is the thought within your mind, and no amount of medicine will be able to help you because it cannot touch the "cause," and can only tinker about with the "effect." Such efforts are on a par with trying to keep the ocean back with a broom.

Therefore when the pain and thought come and seek admittance at the door of your mind, immediately deny their existence, They have no real existence. You, the real YOU, are a perfect mental creature in a perfect mental world, where there is no such thing as pain or "attacks," and if you realize this you can never be ill. It is only when you let thoughts and suggestions of pain and illness come into the mind that pain and illness become possible in your body, because what happens in your body and life is an exact reflex of what you hold in your mind. Therefore if you deny pain and sickness in your perfect Mental World, then at once the pain will cease. In lesson 2 I told you that by denying evil you not only killed the thought of evil, but that you also destroyed the evil itself, and that later you could prove the truth of this. This you can do with pain. If, when in pain, you will rise into your perfect Mental World and deny pain, then the pain will go away almost immediately. After denying pain and sickness, affirm perfect health. The denial will kill the harmful thought and cleanse the mind, and the affirmation will heal and build up and make all future attacks weaker. By this method you can "reverse" every harmful thought, belief and emotion.

It is necessary when you deny any evil, no matter what it may be, that you clearly realize that you are denying apparent evil to exist in the material world. For instance, if you have a carbuncle as big as your fist at the back of your neck it is foolish to deny that it exists, because it does exist as much as anything can he said to exist in this transient world.

There are, however, two YOUS. There is the material YOU, and there is the sublime mental and spiritual YOU. The material YOU is a transient fleeting material person, the real YOU is a glorious mental and spiritual creature, imperishable and eternal. When you (the real YOU) raise yourself into your Perfect World of Mind, you leave the imperfect and coarse material body behind, and it is the sublime YOU, the perfect Mental and Spiritual YOU who, in a perfect World of Infinite Good, Purity and Perfection, deny that there is a carbuncle. You, the sublime YOU, have no carbuncle, it is only the material YOU which you have left behind which has a carbuncle. By raising yourself into your Perfect World of Mind you transfer your consciousness from the material world to that Transcendental World of Infinite Perfection which our greatest philosophers and thinkers have always realized to exist around us and above us. This is why, as gnu raise yourself into your Perfect World of Mind, your pain disappears like the sound of a band dying away in the distance; it is because you have transferred your consciousness from a material world to a mental or spiritual one.

If, when you have entered this Perfect World of Mind you deny the evil that is troubling you (by this you do not deny that it exists in your material body but only in your radiant mental body) and if you then meditate upon the Infinite Perfection Boundless Life, Perfect Good, Unsullied Purity and Immeasurable Power of the Infinite Mind which rules this Perfect Mental World; if you will bask, as it were, in the sunshine and happiness of Infinite Perfection and Love of this Transcendental World, then you open your life and your physical body to the action of the Universal Mind, and your material life, circumstances and body become more like the life of the Perfect World of Mind, and your body more like your sublime mental body. Thus if it is a carbuncle that is troubling you, then it will disperse and your body become quite healthy. The clearer your concept of the Perfect World is the more rapid and certain are the results in your life, body and circumstances.

Every time you rise to your Perfect Mental World and deny evil, every time you realize and bask in the infinite Perfections of the ideal world, each time that you do this, evil is destroyed in your life and body, and good is installed in its place. Therefore, the more you live in your Perfect World the more perfect will your life and circumstances become.

Remember, therefore, to always retire into yourself and to rise into your Perfect World of Mind before making a denial and an affirmation.

MEDITATION NO. 3

To be pondered over between the hours of 6 a. m. and 9 a. m. and 9 p. m. and 11 p. m. Especially just before retiring is recommended.

In the past I have listened to the distracting voices of this imperfect unsatisfying Life of the senses. I have been pulled this way and that, by desire, by impulse, by uncontrolled emotions, and have been influenced by the advice of those who have had no inward knowledge. Henceforth I turn a deaf ear to all these voices and listen only to the inward voice which always speaks with perfect wisdom. No more shall I be perplexed and worried not knowing which way to turn or what to do, instead I shall be guided perfectly by the inward voice of inspiration. I raise my mind above this life of the senses and dwell in the perfect World of Mind. All thoughts and suggestions and states that are not in harmony with the highest good, I reverse into their opposites. Thus do I cleanse my mind, my thought, my life, my circumstances, my world, and build up my life anew.

When perplexed or faced with difficult problems, I retire into my inner self, and, by thought control, I keep out, or "reverse," the unwanted thought, until my inner mind is stilled and calmed, and I car hear the inner voice of wisdom. This voice of wisdom never errs, never leads astray, but always guides me toward the highest good. Therefore I have no worry or care or perplexity, because I always know how to act even in the most perplexing circumstances, being guided perfectly by the inner voice of wisdom.

Henceforth there is for me no care, anxiety or worry, because I am guided into all good. Every good and perfect thing is mine NOW. Health, prosperity, happiness, peace of mind, all are mine here and now.

APPENDIX

Having for this week past impressed on your Subliminal Mind that it CAN think constructively and drawing upon the All-Knowledge, solve your every problem, it is now necessary for you to tell your Subliminal Mind that it DOES solve all your problems. This week's meditation indicates the way--to retire into yourself--this is the secret. To most students it is a difficult task to still the senses and inhibit unwanted thought, but it is comparatively easy, if, instead of trying to inhibit all thought and keep on concentrating upon it and dismissing every thought of care, worry, business, or anything to do with the senses which comes to you. It must be a thought which will draw you away from the life of the senses to the greater life of the mind and spirit. For instance, the Bible student might with advantage concentrate upon some such words as these: "Thou wilt keep him in perfect peace whose mind is stayed on Thee." Another might say with Emerson: "I am the owner of the Sphere, of the seven stars and the Solar Year," and so on according to what your religion or philosophical views may happen to be. Or you can concentrate upon a mental image of infinite beauty and perfection, the future Golden Age, Paradise, Heaven or whatever is to you the highest, MOST PLEASING and most inspiring. Continue to dismiss all other thought until all worry is killed and the mind and Spirit are at rest. Then say in your own words, something like this: My Subliminal Mind draws upon the All-Wisdom and solves my every problem and difficulty.

The life that lies before the student of Truth is one of great glory--of infinite expansion and unfoldment. It does not, however, always appear thus to him. In order to test his mettle, it often appears drab and hopeless. Everything seems to go wrong, and voices whisper "Go back, why trouble any longer, the pursuit is hopeless." If the student does go back he proves that he is not worthy, and for him there can never be the steep ascent to God. But the one who will keep on in spite of all discouragements and opposition, and who proves his worth, passes on to a life of indescribable joy, of victory and achievement, of abundant health and peace of mind.

I affirm for you the life of true freedom. "Ye shall know the Truth, and the Truth shall set you free."

PART IV

WE now have to deal with that part of your Mind which is the center of all action and the seat of all memory. Not only the memory of this life, but the race memory of all mankind.

This division of the mind we will call the sub-conscious mind, we will do so in order to distinguish it from the mind of creation, intuition, and inspiration, which we have already considered, and also from the objective or conscious mind which will be described later.

This sub-division is not orthodox according to the ordinary teachings of psychology. The usual practice is to term the whole of the submerged mind sub-conscious. That this is not correct must, if we think for a moment, be apparent. The sub-conscious mind acts only according to instruction and instinct. Thoughts and commands flow from the seat of the Will through the conscious mind down into the sub-conscious mind and are immediately acted upon. The sub-conscious mind is a blind intelligence. It cannot reason--it can remember, it can act--but it cannot think, plan or reason.

Yet we have a mind within us that can inspire, create, and bring forth the most wonderful thoughts. A mind which can solve our most complicated problems, that can guide us through the most difficult situations if we will but trust it. This cannot be the sub-conscious mind because we have already seen that this is a blind intelligence acting only upon instruction, suggestion and animal instinct. Therefore, there must be a mind or minds other than the sub-conscious, and this I have termed, for the want of a better word, the subliminal.

The sub-conscious mind is a kind of a sleepy giant, or a slumbering volcano. It only requires arousing to cause it to manifest extraordinary power.

It is a vast and wonderful intelligence, so wonderful that our consciousness cannot form any conception of its wonders. All that we know is that this wonderful center of life and action is as far above our understanding as our own consciousness is beyond the comprehension of a beetle.

Yet this sub-conscious mind of ours is subject to our will and guidance. Within us is this wondrous power--the almost infinite intelligence; yet its use and control are in our own hands.

Unto us is given the ability to govern a power whose extent we cannot gauge, to direct an intelligence so great that it is impossible for us to grasp its full significance.

The sub-conscious mind is the center of all action. It is by this mind that everything that we do is accomplished.

It is the personification of tireless energy. It works constantly, it never sleeps; for while WE sleep the sub-conscious mind is busily engaged in repairing and rebuilding the body. Whatever thought we allow to pass into the sub-conscious mind is translated into action. This is why a thought has been described as "an action in the process of being born."

The great lesson for you, dear reader, to learn is this, that if the sub-conscious mind translates each thought into action, then thought control is the one great transcendental fact of life. If you possess the power to control your thoughts, you have at once the power to control your actions. If you can control your actions what a life of possibility opens before you!

One of the principal causes of failure in life is due to inability to control the thoughts. Wrong thoughts each the sub-conscious mind, these are translated into wrong actions and these bring failure and disaster in their train.

When the thoughts are uncontrolled, then the sub-conscious mind will act upon any thought or suggestion that may "float" in.

Now thoughts and suggestions are born not only within the consciousness, they are also received from without. Like a wireless apparatus which receives messages through vibrations in the ether, so does the human mind receive impressions from without.

Thoughts are things, are entities, have form and substance and are eternal. Thoughts impinge upon your consciousness and unless you are able to reject them they will enter the sub-conscious mind and bring forth action in your life and conduct.

If therefore the thought be evil, then evil will result, if of weakness then failure will follow, you cannot prevent the action once you have entertained the thought.

In the same way if you entertain a noble thought, a noble action will result. If thoughts of success and power are dwelt upon, then success and power to accomplish will be manifested in your life, and circumstances. It is thought that rules your life, therefore if you govern your thoughts you control your life.

Suggestion meets you at every turn. Kind friends with the best of motives "suggest" ill-health to you when they remark on your pallor. Their well meant remarks of "How ill you look" send a suggestion of sickness to your sub-conscious mind, which later manifests itself in real sickness in the body.

Articles in your daily paper on diet, Influenza and other topics again suggest illness to you; even the advertisements suggest that you have Kidney disease or worse, and that to save your life it is necessary for you to take certain tablets or pills. The newspapers themselves do their best to suggest evil to you. The columns are full of the seamy sordid side of life. If any man commits a crime, it is reported in the papers. If however he resists temptation and instead does a good deed, no notice is

taken. Therefore newspapers give an entirely false presentation of life. The press closes its eyes to the good and presents the evil and thus suggests evil to you, which if you do not watch it, will produce evil in your life.

For every bad deed reported in the papers, a thousand good actions go unrecorded. The world is full of noble deeds and gracious thoughts, and they can be seen and realized by those who look for them.

Therefore be very careful what newspapers you read and how you read them.

Avoid reading of the evil, seamy side of life; instead, look for the good, and you will find it. When reading your paper devote your attention to the large things, those which will go down in history. Avoid that which is mean and petty--thus will you avoid unwholesome and dangerous suggestion.

Newspapers, periodicals and some books would have you believe that life is an unlovely thing. Even some hymn writers have dared to describe the world as a vale of tears and life as a long drawn out woe. Do not believe these wicked suggestions. Life is a gracious and lovely thing. It is full of beauty and love and peace and happiness. Life is what we make it, we can make it sublime or we can make it savor of Hell. It is in our own hands. Therefore do not read either papers, books or magazines that do not present life in a joyous and optimistic way. Avoid low class scrappy reading. Read instead good books by great minds. Imbibe noble thoughts. Read good poetry if you can. Seek the beautiful, the noble, the true, in your reading and in your fellow men, and you will find them and be richly blest thereby.

"How then," you ask, "can I escape all this harmful suggestion'? I am conscious of evil in my life. I do not know what to expect next. How then can I cast out evil and avoid all these harmful suggestions that impinge upon my consciousness from a thousand different sources?"

The answer is,

BY DENIALS

First of all I want you to understand that your life consists only of that which is in your mind. Your world also is really nothing more than a ref action of your own mind and what is in your own mind. It is because of this that two people in precisely the same circumstances will each find life and the world very different. One will see In life great joy and much cause for thankfulness, and the other may experience only unhappiness and disappointment. The difference is not in circumstances but in the mind. The mind is the real thing, the world is transient and fleeting, and has, philosophically speaking, no REAL existence, but MIND endures.

The natural or "mortal mind" view of life and the world is almost always the exact opposite of what is the real spiritual truth and fact. Metaphysics tell us that the visible world is an inverted reflection of the real. If then it is inverted, it is natural, until our spiritual or inner eyes are opened to the truth, for us to see things as the exact opposite of what they really are. Therefore it is not surprising to find that, whereas the mortal or animal mind of the senses, thinks the world is the real thing and the mind only a shadow, the real TRUTH is, that mind and spirit are real and eternal, and the visible world but a transient and impermanent thing which has no actual reality.

Such being the case then the only thing that really matters is what is in the mind or what is not in the mind. If we have a belief in evil, and thoughts of evil, in our mind, then we have evil in our life. If, however, we can cast the thought of, and belief in, evil out of our mind then it will cease to appear in our life.

By raising ourselves above the sensuous life and realizing our permanent world of Mind and there denying evil, poverty, failure, pain, sickness, unhappiness, or whatever our trouble may be, we kill the thought which is the cause of all our troubles. Then whatever we affirm will take their place. If we deny "evil," then we follow by affirming "good," if we deny sickness, then we affirm prosperity and affluence. By denials we can take out all the evil, care, fear and worry out of our lives and build up in their place by means of affirmations, perfect good, success, affluence, happiness, health, love, peace and courage.

Everything being in the mind, then everything that is taken out of the mind is taken out of the life, and everything that is put into the mind, comes into the life. Thus it is possible with mathematical accuracy and certainty to recreate the life, to cast out all the undesirable and to build up in its place only the beautiful, the good, the true.

Life is what we like to make it. We can make it like heaven itself, full to the brim with all that is good and beautiful, or we can turn it into a perfect hell. Therefore do not accept the suggestions of those, who having failed in life, proceed to call it hard names. We can make life a continual joy, if we create a heaven within us by the quality of our thinking and mental processes. All that we see in life, all that we experience, yea, even life itself, is but the outward expression of the life within. The life within is built up by our thinking.

You will have seen by this time the purpose and value of affirmations.

Affirmations are concentrated thoughts. Back of each affirmation is a strong emotion and this gives it tremendous driving force.

Not only do affirmations impress the sub-conscious mind thus producing action in accordance with the Will, but they project outwards from the mind into space, attract forces and help from other sources and bring them to minister and to bless.

Not only so but they also arouse the subliminal mind to inspire, to create, to impart wisdom.

By the use of affirmations all the finer forces are aroused to action and the life is transformed from weakness or ineffectiveness to strength or purposefulness.

By the use of affirmations, the Will is strengthened until it becomes so strong all else has to bend to it.

By the use of affirmations, the body is strengthened and made healthy, and exercise and body culture become a pleasure instead of a duty.

By the use of affirmations difficult tasks and unpleasant duties become easy of accomplishment.

By the use of affirmations it is possible to break bad habits of a life-long standing, and replace them with good ones.

By the use of affirmations we can build up character, mould our circumstances, shape our destiny, captain our soul, we can be what we will, do whatever we desire attain to all our ideals.

Therefore it is of the utmost importance that you should be most diligent in practicing the affirmations--always. Never let a single night or morning pass without spending several minutes in quiet concentration on the affirmation given you in this course.

Reading this course through will do you but little good, it is DOING what it teaches that is going to make you strong and successful.

Mental and Physical lethargy must be overcome. It is by sustained action that you can accomplish, you cannot dream yourself to success, you have to win it.

Therefore you must concentrate, concentrate, concentrate, upon the affirmations
and visualizing exercises. The latter are form of affirmation and are of equal importance.

A WORD OF WARNING

Do not keep changing your affirmations. Do not affirm one thing one day and another the next; it causes confusion in your mental World, and makes "confusion worse confounded" in your life. Of course as you overcome weaknesses and bad habits you will alter your affirmations accordingly. You will always find some defect that wants eradicating. Otherwise keep to the affirmations given in these lessons.

By this 1: do not mean that you are not to make denials, reversions and affirmations at all times adapted to all the varying circumstances and difficulties of life, because these are, for your own protection, necessary.

Thus, if you see a sight that suggests evil to you, a drunken man, an act of hate, a quarrel, an act of immorality; or if you read that which is lowering and depressing and suggestive of lower things, then, for your own protection, you must reverse it.

For instance if you see an angry violent man, if you do not reverse this, the suggestion of evil conveyed to you by this sight will sink into your sub-conscious mind and cause cells to vibrate in sympathy, thus making YOU more susceptible to anger thoughts, besides lowering the tone of your mind generally. Therefore you must raise yourself to your perfect Mental World and deny anger, by saying, "Man being a perfect mental creature, can never be angry. There is no anger in this perfect world of Mind, all is love and goodwill." By so doing not only will you stop the suggestion of evil from harming you, you will also at the same time make yourself stronger than ever before, and, strange as it may seem to you now, you will reduce the anger in the mind of the angry man. The reason of this is, that there is really only one Mind, we are all inlets of the same sea, and if we cast evil out of our own mind, then we also make the world and the minds of others the better by so doing. Thus by purifying himself does man become a savior of the world.

These reversals of denials and affirmations, made in your perfect World of MIND, must be taking place all day; it is in this way that every evil is transmuted into good, every difficulty into accomplishment, every threat of failure into success, and every pain or sickness or disease thought changed into perfect health. This must go on continually, thus will you grow in power daily.

But apart from this you will doubtless have some plan towards which you are moving. You have some ambition to be realized, some creative purpose in your mind which you wish to accomplish. To attain to this end you deny failure, you affirm success, you visualize a picture of that which you wish to achieve. That being so, and having made up your mind, now STICK TO IT. Do not change your affirmation, do not alter your mental image. KEEP IT UNCHANGED until it is accomplished. If you vary it and change it you will bring the utmost confusion into your life. Therefore do not change, modify or alter the main creative plan of your life, see to it that the image remains unimpaired, getting clearer and more sharply defined from day to day. If you do this you will see it working out with mathematical precision in your life.

This course has been prepared so as to guide students by a sure and safe path to the goal of their ambitions.

It will guide you if you follow the lessons exactly. Therefore while taking this course, do not read any other metaphysical literature. Concentrate on this teaching, persevere with the "doing" of this teaching, and you will be able, like the writer, to prove and demonstrate its truth in yaw life and circumstances.

I want you to start seriously to develop your visualizing powers. By this you will improve your memory out of all knowledge, but that is quite a minor matter. What is of importance is that what you create in the form of a mental vision, if persistently held in the mind, will assuredly manifest itself in your life. Thus you have two methods by which you can alter your life, create better circumstances, and achieve success. 1st, by Denials and Affirmations, and, 2nd, by Meditation, Concentration and Visualizing. The two should work together. For instance, you make an affirmation, preceded by a denial, next, you conjure up a mental picture of what you have affirmed yourself to be.

You wish to be successful, therefore first of all you must deny evil and affirm Good, because evil is the general cause of all your troubles and lack of success; next you will affirm Success and follow this by visualizing either yourself in your perfect mental world, radiant and successful, or else dwell only on the perfect world of MIND where there is no failure or limitation of any description.

First you clear away the mist of evil which clouds your vision and numbs your faculties and crowds your life with difficulty, this you do by killing it by the use of the denial "There is no evil." Use this denial until the mist clears away and you get a clear view of your perfect world of Mind, then affirm "There is only Infinite Good." Then deny poverty and failure, because they have no part in a perfect world, neither can they affect you, who are in essence, a perfect mental creature.

Having killed failure and poverty by denial, then affirm "I am Success, I am a perfect mental creature, one with the Source of all Good, part of the Universal Mind." "I am Success, like a magnet I attract to me all that I need." "A thousand invisible forces hasten to do my bidding." I am carried along by an irresistible power, I am Success, Success, Success.

Make this affirmation preceded by the denials, night and morning, always making the affirmation in "Your perfect mental world," buttress it up by repeating it during the day, each time raising yourself to your higher world; do this, and you will revolutionize your life.

In order to increase your powers of mental imagery, do the following exercise:

Take a simple flower, or picture, and gaze at it very attentively for several minutes. Examine it in every possible way. Impress every detail upon your mind, then close your eyes and call up an exact mental image of the thing you have been looking at. If the image is crisp and sharply defined with no details missing you will have done well, if not, keep on trying until you succeed.

When you go into a strange room or office examine carefully every detail; where each piece of furniture is, what pictures are on the walls, what is on the floor, the kind of fireplace and everything else that forms part of the furnishing. After you get home or when in the train, close your eyes and recall, by making a mental image, as much as you can, of what you saw. Practice this visualizing as much as possible during the coming week, and make affirmations to suit your growing developments. Whatever your need may be, you can make a denial and affirmation to supply that need. Whatever difficulty you have to face you can overcome it by denial and affirmation made in your perfect World of Mind.

This course seeks first to build a firm foundation of character upon which you can later erect the superstructure of success. Seek first to eradicate all weaknesses of character and in their place install their opposites. For instance, if you have been a procrastinator, become instead noted for your instant action. If you have been pessimistic, become cheerful and optimistic instead. If unpunctual, become the most punctual person who ever lived. If you have been sullen and morose, seek to be bright and cheerful. All this is possible and really quite easy of accomplishment, by the use of denials, affirmations and mental imagery.

When you have built up your character, the road of success will become comparatively easy, because success is principally a matter of character.

The elementary general affirmation has now served its purpose and must now be strengthened. You have progressed sufficiently to join us in the greatest denial and affirmation of all, which is

There is NO EVIL
Only INFINITE GOOD

It is very difficult for the beginner to realize that "There is no evil." There are entities in your mind which prevent you from understanding this truth, but they will be cast out by the denial. So powerful is this denial that it makes some people quite ill at first. But this only proves how great is the cleansing work that is going on in the depths of the mind. Keep on making the denial night and day; keep looking up into your perfect world of mind, and after a time you will suddenly realize that FOR YOU there is no evil, only Infinite Perfection and everything that is beautiful and true. Precede every other affirmation by this denial and affirmation. Before starting any important work make use of them; and previous to engaging in any meditation, always use them; raising, at the same time, your mind into its perfect world.

By this means you will so cleanse and strengthen your mind that you will transform your life.

For meditation this week think upon these words of James Allen:

"The soul that is impure, sordid and selfish, is gravitating with unerring precision toward misfortune and catastrophe; the soul that is pure, unselfish, and noble, is gravitating with equal precision toward happiness and prosperity. Every soul attracts its own, and nothing can come to it that does not belong to it. To realize this is to recognize the Universality of Divine Law."

And also upon these words of Buddha:

"All that we are is the result of what we have thought; it is founded on our thoughts; it is made up of our thoughts."

And again, these further words of James Allen: "Your own thoughts, desires and aspirations comprise your world, and, to you, all that there is in the Universe of beauty and joy and bliss, or of ugliness and sorrow and pain, is contained within yourself. By your own thoughts you make or mar your life your world, your Universe." Referring to page 92 of this lesson, third paragraph from the bottom, it should be stated that quicker results will be obtained if in addition to visualizing yourself radiantly successful, you will create a sharply defined picture of the exact success that you wish to achieve. If it is money that you want then "see" the money falling in showers upon your desk, if it is service to others that you desire, then "see" yourself nursing the sick and ministering to the broken-hearted, whatever you picture in this way persistently, will, in time, be brought to pass in your life. Nothing ever "happens," it is always "brought to pass." You cannot get what you want merely by a pious wish, you have to work for it by mental imagery, then in time the way will open for you in a most marvelous manner.

Continue to practice concentration on one thought or mental image, inhibiting all ether thoughts until the senses are entirely stilled. Then say as before: "My Subliminal Mind draws upon the All-Wisdom and solves my every problem."

PART V

THE Objective or Conscious Mind is the outer or surface mind of mind. It is the finite mind of very close limitations. It receives impressions through the organs of sight, hearing, taste, touch and smell. It learns from books, speech, experience and experiment.

We have seen that the subliminal mind is one with the Infinite Mind of the Universe, differing only in degree and not in kind, yet this is useless if the objective mind does not make use of the potential powers lying dormant within.

We have also seen that the so called sub-conscious mind is pregnant with tremendous power, and that it is a wonderful intelligence far exceeding anything that the objective consciousness can grasp or understand. Further that this is regulated and controlled by thoughts, impressions and suggestions, coming through the conscious mind. Therefore this great intelligence is ruled and governed, or ought to be, by the objective mind. Yet of what use is all this if the mind of the senses does not govern wisely or does not govern at all, but lets the sub-conscious mind run amuck, as it were, and acting upon instincts and false impressions, untruths and harmful suggestions, turn the whole life into an inferno of trouble and difficulty?

Therefore you will see that the objective mind, although very limited, is, in a way, the most important of all, at any rate as far as this life and consciousness are concerned, for through it the Ego governs or can govern the whole of the submerged mind.

The Ego is the "I" part of man. It is his personal individual inner self.

The real "YOU" is your individual Ego. The real "YOU" within is seeking expression through your minds and then through your brain and body and outer life.

It can only do this properly when the Will is strong enough either to carry out, or force your minds to carry out, the commands of the Ego.

Suppose the real inner "YOU" says to the Will: I wish to succeed in this undertaking. We will imagine that "this undertaking" is a course of study which requires a great deal of application and perseverance, and a certain amount of sacrifice of pleasure for its accomplishment. It necessitates working while others are playing, the resisting of entreaties on the part of friends to join them in their pleasures.

After receiving its instruction, the Will passes on the order through the conscious to the sub-conscious mind, but unless your Will is naturally very strong it does this in a half-hearted manner. Although this supposed course of study is of the utmost importance, for without it you cannot succeed in your profession or calling, yet the Will is so weak it cannot impress this sufficiently upon the sub-conscious mind, with the result that there is very little driving force behind your efforts.

For a time the studies go along successfully. For one thing the first lessons are always easy, and for another, there is the novelty and freshness of the new work, and the glow of self-satisfaction at having entered upon a self-appointed task.

But after a time the tasks get more difficult and require more application and concentration, the calls of friends to join them in their pleasures become more insistent, and the Will not being strong can no longer deal with the situation. The Will, through weakness, allows suggestions such as "the task is too difficult," "others are enjoying life why should not you?" "others can get on in life without working themselves to death, so why not you?" to pass down into the sub-conscious mind. The latter knowing no better and acting entirely upon suggestion, responds accordingly, with the result that the lessons are flung aside, games are indulged in instead, and another failure is written large on the scroll of your life.

Suppose on the other hand that your Will has been reinforced by affirmations. First, the sub-conscious mind is deeply impressed. It realized that this self imposed task has to be accomplished somehow, no matter what the cost may be in hard work, perseverance, discomfort and self-sacrifice. Therefore from the very first there is great driving power put behind your efforts. A concrete well-defined image of the object of your endeavor, the successful ending of your studies, the pride of achievement, the pleasure it will give your friends, the great assistance it will be to you in your profession, the increased status, the enlarged income, the better house, the improved condition of living for those dependent upon you, all these combined in one sharply defined image, are impressed upon the sub-conscious mind so deeply that they form a pattern upon which the mind will concentrate all its intense energies, activities and powers. The energies and powers of the mind working on definite lines laid down by the Will, create in the life a complete replica of the image which has been held in the mind.

When studies become difficult, instead of faltering, the mind puts forth greater effort, generates more power, and overcomes the subject of difficulty. When friends try to entice you to leave your task and join them in their pleasure, then entreaties fall upon deaf ears. You reply, "I must complete this course of study," or "I must pass this examination," "when I have succeeded and won the position I seek, then, and not until then, I will unbend a little."

This is why very few men succeed and many fail. Most men have not the staying power to succeed. They have the desire to succeed but they lack the force of character, and the necessary will-power to carry their plans to fruition. Some men are full of splendid ideas, but they never carry them out. They see their opportunities, but lack the strength to take advantage of them.

Such a man always has plenty of excuses for his non-success--any reason but the right one. He will never admit that it was his Will that failed. Circumstances, he tells you, were against him. Nobody would help him at the critical moment. Something or other "happened," which accounted for his failure.

And so it was that he gave up his little business, just at the moment when it needed but a little push to get it past the corner and on the road to a permanent success. Now he works for another man and for the rest of his life will be a servant and nothing but poverty and the workhouse to look forward to in his old age. The number of men endowed with the necessary strength of will to succeed by will-power alone, is comparatively small. For one who can succeed in this way there are thousands who must fail. These thousands of failures might be turned into successes if they only realized the Power within them, and understood the wonders than can be wrought from affirmations, and mental imagery. Men and women endowed with but the ordinary amount of will-power can achieve success beyond their wildest dreams when they have learnt to use their true Inward Powers, and to reinforce their Wills by the use of affirmations and mental imagery.

But it must not be thought that because you are being taught valuable metaphysical knowledge that you can neglect your Will. On the contrary the training of the Will is of the utmost importance.

In order to succeed you need imagination and vision--faith in yourself and the power within you--but more than all else, staying power is required, and this is largely dependent upon the strength of the Will.

Desire to succeed, energy, ambition, ability, intellect, imagination, capacity, large ideas, all are good, all vitally necessary for the achievement of success, but they are all useless if "staying power" is lacking. If the will is weak then nothing can be accomplished.

Therefore one of the primary objects of this Course is the building up within you of that staying power, that strength of purpose, that stability of character, that inflexibility of Will, that are necessary for the achievement of the highest success.

While it teaches valuable metaphysical knowledge which gives you a tremendous advantage in life, because it reveals to you your inward powers, and shows you how to use them, yet these powers and forces have to be controlled by your Will, otherwise they may work harm instead of good.

Do not misunderstand me, I do not teach that, except in a very few cases, success can be won by will-power alone. It is not will-power that creates, inspires and attracts success. It is the subliminal mind that is the fountain of perpetual power and the storehouse of wisdom. It is the sub-conscious mind that provides the driving power, but it is the Will that provides the staying power.

The Ego decides what is to be done. It is the Will that compels the sub-conscious mind to carry out the wishes of the Ego. It is not the will that executes, it is the power of the sub-conscious mind. All other systems of instruction with which I am acquainted teach a series of gymnastics for the objective mind, and a kind of Will training by brute force. It is a joyless quest-seeking success along these lines. It is equivalent to trying to start an automobile engine with the petrol turned off, or without first switching on the electric current.

"Scientific Thought" arouses the latent powers within, puts the student in touch with all the Cosmic Forces, and trains the Will in order to direct them towards the accomplishment of his ambitions.

The ordinary and time-honored way of trying to develop the Will by brute force is almost always unsuccessful, and, even when it succeeds, is an extremely slow and painful method.

In this course of lessons the strength of the Will grows almost imperceptibly. All the affirmations and exercises if done systematically and thoroughly will strengthen your will-power out of all knowledge. If you will pay great attention to the affirmations and persevere with the visualizing you will find that your will-power will increase to such an extent that you will become a new creature. Therefore pay the greatest attention to these things so that your will-power may increase and its development keep pace with your increase of knowledge.

Affirmations rob the training of the Will of half its terrors. If you affirm calmly and steadily and confidently that you will perform some difficult or unpleasant duty at a certain time, you will find, when the time comes, that there will be an impulse urging you to perform that duty. And when you screw up your courage and go and do the thing you dread or dislike, you find to your surprise that it is not half as difficult or unpleasant as you thought it would be.

This is the power of the sub-conscious mind. It not only urges you to act at the proper time, it also supplies you with the power to act. It must be pointed out here that when the sub-conscious mind gives you this impulse, it must be obeyed. If, we will say, you have affirmed, both over night and early in the morning, that at 3 p. m. you will go into your chief's office and ask for a raise of salary, then when the time arrives go and do it. Fear will say, "he is very stern, unpleasant man and will only snap your head off--put it off for another day." Instead of listening to the voice of fear, deny it, and say, "there is no fear, man is a perfect mental creature and can know no fear," then affirm "I am courageous and fear no man," "I am Success. I attract Success by the Infinite Power within me," and buoyed up by this, go and see the man at once. You will find him far easier to deal with than you expected. If you do not get the raise, you may pave the way for it, or by finding out why your request is refused, you may be able to make a raise possible in the near future. In any case you have done yourself good, you have strengthened your Will, and lost your fear of a man you formerly rather dreaded. If, however, you listen to the voice of fear, and put the dreaded interview off until the morrow, you do yourself a grievous harm.

If you affirm that you are going to do a certain act, and then do not do it, even when your faithful sub-conscious mind gives you the helpful impulse, then you are destroying your mental powers root and branch. You are deliberately slamming the door of progress and achievement in your own face.

If you have an alarm clock, and set it to act at a certain time in the morning, and then get up directly its bell rings, that clock will always awaken you. If, on the other hand, you turn over when the bell rings and go to sleep again instead. of rising, then never again will you be able to hear the clock ring. As an alarm clock it will be useless.

So it is with the sub-conscious mind. When it prompts, obey it, for if you do not, it will soon cease its promptings, and this wonderful power will be lost to you.

So you see that by the use of affirmations you can so influence the powers within you that things impossible to you before become comparatively easy of accomplishment. The only condition being that you act with decision--that you go fearlessly forward and do exactly what you have planned to do.

Now I want you from this time forward to do each day something that is unpleasant or difficult but which you really ought to do.

It may be that you really ought to go to your dentist, you are aware that your teeth are getting rapidly worse and that the dentist could stop the mischief if he were given the opportunity, thus saving you much pain, loss and ultimate expense. You know that your digestion, and consequently your general health, are suffering through this neglect and yet you keep putting the matter off. It means the trouble of arranging appointments, the sacrifice of a certain amount of time, and the expenditure of money; also, it is unpleasant to say the least, so you have been letting the matter drift.

Or it may be that there is a certain man you ought to go and interview. You know that if you could get him interested a lot of profitable business would follow. You have, however, put off visiting him from time to time because he is a great man and has an antipathy to people such as yourself. You know that if you do see him you will most probably be snubbed most unmercifully, and that no business will result. For these two reasons you have avoided what promises to be an unpleasant interview.

Whatever the unpleasant duty may be that you decide to perform, you should prepare the way by denials and affirmations.

For your visit to your dentist you can deny and affirm as follows: "There is nothing to fear at the dentist; there is nothing that he can do to me that I cannot take smiling." Therefore tomorrow at 11 a. m. I will write (or 'phone) for an appointment with Mr. ——. He will put my mouth in splendid order and this will benefit my health.

After saying the affirmation over several times, visualize a picture of yourself in your office. You see yourself look at the clock on your desk. It is 11 o'clock. You see yourself take up the telephone and ring up Mr. —— and hear yourself arrange an appointment. Or you see yourself dash off a note to your dentist asking for an appointment.

Next, you picture yourself in perfect health and your mouth in splendid order.

The next day you will have no difficulty in carrying out what you have affirmed.

If it is a difficult interview that you decide to undertake, make the affirmation for three or even seven days if possible before the interview takes place. Proceed as follows: Raise yourself up mentally into your perfect World of Mind and deny fear. Say: "I am a perfect radiant mental creature, I am one with the Infinite Universal Mind, therefore I am full of courage. No one can make me afraid." On —— day at noon (or any other time you can arrange) I will interview Mr. ——. He will hear what I have to say and the result of the interview will be satisfactory to me. I do this not by hypnotic power which is evil, not by mind domination, but by the Law of Attraction." After affirming in the usual way, visualize your interview. Imagine yourself engaged in conversation with Mr. ——, who seems interested in what you are saying. See yourself entirely at ease and quite natural in your manner. See yourself making a satisfactory end to your interview. Do this very earnestly every night and morning until the interview takes place. When it does take place you will find it will be more satisfactory than ever you had dared hope.

When you have learned in this way to act with courage and decision, you can leave off using affirmations for such small matters and use them for more important things.

As you progress in Scientific Thinking you will find wonderful possibilities opening up before you, so that you will always find a use for all the time that you can devote to denials and affirmations. As you advance in knowledge and power, you can transfer your affirmations to more difficult problems, Your character is constantly growing in strength and virility, and things that were impossible at one time become easy of accomplishment, but always front of you lie fresh fields to conquer; there is no limit to the life of the Mind.

Before every affirmation, make the great mind cleansing denial, "There is no evil," and its complementary affirmation, "Only infinite good." Every time that you make use of these you have taken something evil out of your life and in its place put something good. If you use them a hundred times a day it will not be too many. You cannot use them too much.

The visible world is described by some deep thinkers and metaphysicians as "heaven obscured by a mist of matter and evil, through which it is seen but faintly and falsely." If this is so, and it is to a certain extent true, then every time that you make use of this great cleansing denial and affirmation you disperse some of the mist, so that you can see heaven a little more clearly. Be this as it may, it is certainly true that the use of the denial of evil and the affirmation of good, do indeed remove evil and replace by good, so that life becomes happier, brighter, more prosperous, and harmonious; even the flowers and trees and our fellow creatures become far more beautiful and lovable than ever before. The world and life are surpassingly beautiful, but not if you view them with a jaundiced eye. If life and the world are not entrancingly lovely to you it is because your eyes are obscured by a mist of evil, or your mind is clouded so that you cannot perceive and understand.

If you will deny evil and affirm good at every possible moment, you will, every time you do so, make the beauty and grandeur of life and the loveliness of the world more apparent to your senses. If you will persevere day after day and week after week and month after month you will come to that stage when you will see things as they are, face to face; you will then be unable to find any words with which to express the glories which you behold. And not only do beauty and loveliness, happiness, joy and content, come through the denial of evil, and the affirmation of good, but the same thing applies to circumstances. Poor or difficult or unpleasant circumstances are all evil. Poverty, lack and want, are, like disease, quite foreign to that which we know as "good." By the denial of evil we cast out all these undesirable conditions from our lives, and by the affirmation of "good" we attract into our lives true success and prosperity and freedom from every kind of lack and limitation.

Every time we do this we make our lives a little better. It is by constant and continual use that we not only stem the tide of evil but make progress in the right direction. Therefore the denial: "There is no evil," and the affirmation, "Only Infinite Good," should be as much a part of your life as breathing.

Continue with the same general affirmation and visualizing exercises, and make your own denials and affirmations as you need them every hour of the day.

MEDITATION

Take a simple flower. Examine it carefully. Note its purity and sweet loveliness. All poets, who have ever lived, have never been able to describe, adequately, its beauty and fresh purity. This flower is an expression of the Universal Life of Mind, as I am an expression of the Universal Life of Mind, therefore we are brothers and sisters. There is only one Life, one Mind--the Universal, and I and this flower are but individual expressions of that Life and Mind.

This flower is a messenger from the Unseen. It tells me that there is no evil. The intelligence that produced this lovely emblem cannot be evil, cannot produce evil, therefore there is no evil, per se, only that which exists in my own animal mind.

Therefore I hear the voice of the flower say in silvery accents: "There is no evil, only infinite Good." And I am content.

APPENDIX

Continue to practice concentration upon one thought or image to the exclusion of all other thoughts and images until the mind is perfectly calm. When you have thoroughly mastered this, and NOT before, you may begin to make use of this wonderful intelligence which you have harnessed to your service. This is explained fully in Lesson XI but in order that you may start getting results at once the following instruction is given: Just as you are falling asleep, calm and still the mind in the manner shown and when you have succeeded, bring your problem before your mind and affirm that while you sleep your Subliminal Mind will solve your problem and give you the answer in the morning. Next dismiss the matter from your mind and go to sleep. In the morning, when you are awake, refuse to worry about your problem or engage in nerve-racking thought about it; instead still the mind as before and the answer will come. If you have been an early student of the Bible it may come in the form of a text; if you have been brought up on proverbs and worldly wisdom it may come in the form of some wise old saying, or, to some, it may come in the form of a whisper. The more you practice this, and make use of this faculty, the clearer and more certain will be the results.

Read this lesson over as often as you can find time to do so; it cannot be absorbed all at once.

Hold in your mind a sharp definite picture of the success you have planned. If it is money that you desire, then see money in abundance pouring in streams on to your desk. If it is health that you need, hold a picture of perfect health ever before your mental eyes. If it is a wealthy practice, then mentally "see" yourself in a perfectly appointed office receiving wealthy clients in large numbers, and "see" them waiting patiently in queues for their turn to see you. Whatever it is that you desire, no matter whether it be invention, genius, love, friends, house, lands or service to others, picture it very definitely and distinctly and hold this image over before your mind, keep constantly calling it up, and every time that you do so let the sight thrill you with pleasure. As you call up the picture affirm "I am Success," and believe that it is already yours. Keep on affirming success, and visualizing success, and it will surely come and in much larger volume than ever you imagined possible.

I wish you the highest possible success.

PART VI

THE Objective or conscious mind is the mind of the senses. It learns from books, persons, experience and experiments. It reasons on things learnt, and on thoughts received from a variety of sources,: and having passed judgment, rejects some things as error, and accepts others as truth. Things considered to be truth are passed down into the sub-conscious mind to add to its existing store of memory and experiences.

Whatever is passed to the sub-conscious mind becomes translated into action. Thus if immoral or impure thoughts are entertained, then immediately physical changes take place in the body, which are simply these thoughts being translated into action by the sub-conscious mind. Thus if one repeatedly imbibes this class of thought, a time arrives when one is compelled by the sub-conscious mind to indulge in immoral practices. This is why many people who have been all their lives apparently quite moral, and well behaved, suddenly break out into flagrant immorality. It is a great surprise and causes great distress to relations and friends. They think that it is a sudden transformation, or that it is due to a certain temptation, or to the evil influence of a certain wicked person. It is instead none of these things. It is simply the result of evil thinking. Evil thoughts produce evil actions. Evil thoughts also attract other thoughts just as evil as themselves. In the same way a person who indulges in evil thinking, attracts other people of similar character.

There is a law running through the Universe which is that "like attracts like," and the operation of this law is unalterable. Think evil thoughts, and you will assuredly attract others just as evil, which will help to drag you down. If a man thinks evil thoughts he will become evil in word and deed. Let him think evil thoughts and he will attract other people even worse than himself. In the same way if you entertain thoughts of failure, if you doubt your ability to succeed, if you feel that circumstances will arise which will "swamp" your business, then you will attract streams of "failure" thoughts which will help to keep success away. Not only so, but you will attract other people of a similar nature, whose pessimism will help to complete your final discomfiture. Like always attracts like. Thus it is that "failures" always drift together, just as men of a successful type always draw to themselves others of the same type of mind. "Birds of a feather flock together" has behind it an unalterable law.

It is the same law that makes it impossible to think or fear sickness, disease or ill-health, without drawing to yourself streams of thoughts of, a similar nature which cause certain cells to vibrate in the sub-conscious mind, and thus produce disease. And not only by so thinking do you produce disease, . but you also attract diseased people to you, who help by their "diseased mental outlook" to make your illness become more firmly seated.

The reverse is of course equally true. If you entertain "pure" thoughts you will attract thoughts of a similar kind from out the ether, and be strengthened and blessed thereby. By the same law you will attract other people of lofty minds who will aid you in your upward climb.

If you entertain beautiful thoughts, you will draw to yourself a constant stream of thoughts of a like nature, and you will attract to yourself friends of a noble and inspiring character.

In the same way, if you allow thoughts of success only to be held in the mind, and chase away all thoughts of failure, you will attract to yourself a full measure of successful thoughts. These will strengthen your determination and inspire you to greater effort. By the same law you will also attract to yourself men and women of a successful type of mind. You will find yourself sought after by successful people, and they will bring with them opportunities for your more abundant success.

Again, if you will only think thoughts of Health and Perfection, and kill by denial all thoughts of disease, if you will raise yourself into your Perfect World of Mind, and realize that there is no such thing as sickness, illness, ill-health or disease, but that instead there is only infinite Perfection and abounding Health, then not only will Health manifest itself in your body, but you will also attract to yourself, happy, radiant, healthy minded, and healthy bodied people, who will inspire and help you in every department of your life.

Therefore you will readily see how important it is that only the right type of thoughts should be allowed to enter the sub-conscious mind.

The Will and the Conscious Mind stand as sentinels at the door of the sub-conscious mind. To them is given the important task of deciding what shall, or what shall not, enter. Every kind of thought and suggestion, inimical to our welfare, meet us and strike us on every hand. Harmful thoughts seek to enter our minds at every turn. Books, magazines, race thought, the mental outlook of friends and acquaintances are all against our mental development. The attitude of mind of the average person, of the common ruck, is not inspiring. It does not suggest "success," it expresses at best, only a passive acceptance of life. It takes like as it is, things as they come. It is not often that you meet a man who is conscious that he is "Master of his fate, the Captain of his soul."

How then can you escape all this deadening, destroying mental atmosphere?

FIRST. You must, in habit of thought, separate yourself from "the crowd." You must shut out their pessimistic-belief-in-circumstances--weak-failure-low-lewd type of thoughts altogether, and live in an entirely different world--the inner world of your own creative thought. If you meet a noble or inspiring thought--and later you will be the recipient of a continuous stream of the finest thoughts the world has ever known--let it in.

I do not mean that you are to look down upon your fellows, for nothing is more destructive or contemptible. You must mix with your fellows, and while holding yourself proof against low and weak types of thought, seek to raise their minds by your own hopeful suggestions. When a friend talks as though failure were a possibility in his life, suggest instead that success is hastening his way. When people are sad, try to cheer them by hopeful suggestions. When they look on the dark side of life, show them the bright side. When they rail and rave, pour oil on the troubled waters. Seek to cheer people up and resolutely refuse to accept the suggestions of their minds.

The greatest antidote to this deadening atmosphere of doubt and helplessness, of ignorance and materialism, of fear and failure, due to the world's wrong habit of thought is the use of that mind cleansing denial "There is no evil." It goes right to the root of all trouble and failure, all that is undesirable in our lives, and destroys it.

The word "evil" embraces everything in life that is not of the highest good; failure, poverty, fear, sickness, disease, pain, ill-health, unhappiness; all that limits, con fines, cramps and fetters one's life, all these and much more are included in this one word. By this denial, all this evil atmosphere is neutralized, and the mind is cleansed, ready for the affirmation "Only Infinite Good" and these two words "Infinite Good" cover everything that we can possibly desire. Peace, Power, Plenty, Health, Happiness and Joy; Success, Achievement, Love, Service to all mankind, what more can one desire?

Therefore mix with your fellows, they are your brothers and sisters; seek to do all the good that you can, but continually cleanse your mind and thought by the use of the denial of evil, and build up your character and life and circumstances by affirmations of Infinite Good.

Thus while you are still mixing with the ordinary everyday type of men--and they have much that is lovable and noble in their characters--yet you will be as the poles apart. The fact that you are taking this. Course proves that you are not as others. That you are taking a course of metaphysical training shows that you are of a different type to the ordinary crowd, that you are marked out for distinction and progress.

SECOND. Everything that you read must be examined and criticized. You must remember that books, papers, magazines, letters, unless you consciously prevent them, will convey suggestions to your sub-conscious mind and in course of time become translated into action. Therefore if you read books of passion your life will be unbalanced and perhaps wrecked by gusts of violent desire, which call loudly to be satisfied. On the other hand, if you will read books written by lofty minds, you will receive thoughts which inspire and strengthen you.

You should therefore choose your reading wisely. Read the best literature, and do not then accept as Truth all that you read. Refuse resolutely to accept any idea that is not in agreement with your new conception of life. All ideas of man being the puppet of powers outside himself, of being the sport of fate and the victim of circumstances must be rigorously rejected. All that tends to strengthen your new conception of life, which is, that all things are delivered into your hands, and that you have the power to conquer both yourself and all difficulty and thus make your life sublime--all that tends to strengthen this mental attitude should be accepted.

The Will and the Conscious Mind stand at the gate; by them you must examine every thought, every suggestion. Hold everything up and examine it in the light of your newly found knowledge, and if it cannot stand this searching test, cast it from you. You can never be successful if you allow thoughts of weakness or failure or fear to enter your sub-conscious mind. The one great outstanding characteristic that distinguishes successful men from the unsuccessful, is their absolute belief and faith in their own ability to succeed. Thoughts of failure, or fear, never enter the mind of the truly successful man. If you examine the character of any great and truly successful man, you will find this dominating characteristic--absolute faith in his own success, and with it an entire absence of fear or weakness.

Therefore it is certain that you can never be successful if you allow doubt and fear to enter your mind; it is only when by mind control you have cast out fear and doubt that you can enter the path that leads to success.

Some men are successful and are not conscious of the laws which govern success, They unconsciously work according to law--by instinct rather than knowledge. It is because they are naturally men of LARGE FAITH and UNFAILING COURAGE that they have become successful.

Therefore you, too, in order to succeed, must have a large faith and unfailing courage. Faith in the power within you and a courage that is born of knowledge. Thus can you be placed on the same footing as that of any other successful man, in fact you will be better equipped than the naturally successful man, for possessing knowledge will enable you to avoid many errors, into which he, through ignorance of the law, might fall.

Therefore in your reading you must close your eyes to all suggestions which are antagonistic to your newly found knowledge.

THIRD. By denial and affirmation you create a new mental outlook.

By denial we obtain immediate relief from our troubles. For instance, if, when you are in pain you will deny that there is pain in your perfect mental World and raise yourself above the ordinary life of the senses, and realize that you, your higher mental self, are a perfect mind, or mental creature, incapable of being attacked by pain, then the pain will quickly go. In the same way whatever trouble may confront you, by denial you obtain immediate relief. Denial kills the evil thought which is the cause of all the trouble, and cleanses and purifies the mind, making it ready for the affirmation.

Always precede an affirmation by the necessary denial. If you are going to affirm health, then first deny ill-health, sickness and disease. If you are going to affirm success, first deny failure, if you wish for prosperity and plenty, then first deny poverty and want, so as to get the mind ready for the affirmation "I am success; prosperity and plenty are already mine."

But, you exclaim, how can I truthfully affirm that I am that which I know myself not to be? The answer is: There are two YOUS. There is the finite, outside, surface, material YOU, and there is the great and glorious inner spiritual and mental being which is the real YOU. The former is a weak and coarse reflection of the latter. This glorious and real YOU is perfect and lives in a perfect mental world. When you affirm in your perfect Mental World, that you are perfect you mean the real and sublime YOU, and you are telling the truth. Whatever good quality you affirm is quite true, because you (yourself, the real YOU) are perfect. By denial of evil and imperfection and by the affirming of infinite perfection you destroy evil in your material life and bring it more into harmony with the perfect life. Therefore what you affirm in your perfect mental world, is later, and sometimes instantaneously, manifested in your material world.

An affirmation has been described by one writer as "a statement of Truth consciously used so as to become the directing power of Life's expression." This is a good and true definition. Scientists will tell you that the submerged mind of man acts only upon suggestion. So powerful is the hidden mind and so subject is it to suggestion that we have in affirmations a weapon of extraordinary power for good, and in negative suggestion a terrible power for evil.

When we use an affirmation we make a statement of Truth which, if repeated often enough, will sink down into the recesses of our mind and become part of our very life. It will galvanize the hidden forces of our mind into activity and guide them into the path of achievement.

If in the past you have been a failure, then by constantly affirming "I am Success," you will gradually eradicate the weak-fearing-give-up-too-soon attitude of your material mind, and build up in its place the mental outlook of courage, cheerfulness, optimism and belief in your ability to succeed.

Failure or lack of success in life is not, as I have already pointed out, due to outward circumstances, but is simply a weakness of character. By affirmations you can build up your character and make its former weak points strongest in your armor.

It is by affirmations, then, that man can control himself, build up his character and shape his own destiny.

It was for this reason that I gave you in your first lesson the affirmation, which is a denial and affirmation combiner, "The old life is dead, I have entered the new life of Success and Power." In that affirmation if consciously applied and persevered with, you kill the old life of failure and partial success, and step out definitely into a new life of power and accomplishment. As a consequence, you will look upon life in a different way, you will act in a different manner, you will attract a different kind of people. Soon you begin to see evidences of the truth of these teachings manifested in your life and circumstances.

Therefore you can by affirmations make yourself proof against the harmful suggestions that meet you on every hand.. By affirmations you build up the courageous, confident, hopeful, cheerful, absolutely certain attitude of mind, which is the only type of mind that can readily succeed.

As you begin to see evidences of the working of your newly found power, you feel lifted up in a strange and wonderful way. You feel as if you are being carried forward, by invisible powers, to success; it is as though some impelling force were pushing you in the back and urging you forward to the goal of your endeavor.

Therefore, persist and persevere with your affirmations. Continue to look for difficult tasks, and unpleasant, but very necessary duties, and aided by the power of affirmations. DO THEM.

Make affirmations to suit your own peculiar needs. If you are too energetic and inclined to run yourself to pieces, and rush and tear about and get your own nerves and everybody's else, on edge, affirm as follows: "I am perfectly calm, cool and collected. I refuse to get excited or flustered. I work quietly and methodically." Then mentally picture yourself at work in a very calm, cool and collected way, without hurry, fluster or excitement. You will find your work go much better in consequence, and certainly not less quickly.

If, on the other hand, you are inclined to be lazy or lethargic, affirm as follows: "I am the personification of industry and energy. I am busy from morning until night." Then picture yourself hard at work, doing good work and plenty of it. This you will find will help you vastly in enabling you to "stick" to your task, and to keep sticking to it day after day.

Thus you have within your grasp the power by which you can overcome every weakness of character; a key which will unlock every door; an art which is the open sesame to the unlimited treasure house of the Universal Mind.

By the use of this wonderful power you can turn failure into success, sorrow into joy, sickness into health, mediocrity into genius. To you all things are possible--strength of purpose, the joy of achievement, all the glories of a life of self-mastery.

Unto you it is given to taste of the delights of heaven while yet upon earth--for heaven and hell are within you, they are but mental states.

Unto him who attains to the dazzling height of self-mastery, unto him who can stand erect, and unafraid, and untroubled by the things that vex and rend the hearts of men; unto him who is master of his passions, his emotions, his circumstances and his life; unto such a one has come that for which the world has longed and strived in vain, about which philosophers, poets and seers have, for centuries, spoken and written, and yet never have been able to grasp or to hold.

He who overcomes himself, overcomes the world; all its treasures are poured at his feet; "all the Divine Forces hasten to minister to his eternal joy." Dear reader, all this is for yon. Persevere with the affirmations and practice the visualization exercises as taught in this course, and you can never fail to succeed beyond your wildest dreams.

For visualizing exercises, picture the window frame of your bedroom, trace the wood of which it is made, step by step, process by process, right back to its original form, the tree in the forest. See clearly and distinctly every stage, leave out no detail.

MEDITATION

In future I am going to close my eyes to the imperfections of other people and endeavor only to see their good points. Everyone has lovable traits in his or her character. Even the hardest "case" has a "soft spot" somewhere, therefore in future I will look only for the lovable traits and the "soft spots." In everyone I shall see something to admire and reverence, something to love.

And I shall not stop with people. I will also look for the good in every circumstance, in every difficulty, in every failure. I will look for the good in every blade of grass and every opening flower, in the wind that blows and the sun that burns my cheek. Rain or sunshine, fair weather or foul, I will see good in everything, see perfection underlying all. Out of these will grow a new sympathy, a more extensive and embracing love, a larger and wider consciousness, for everyone and everything are my brothers, each forms a part of the one whole, we are one with one another and the Universal Life and Mind of which we each form an individual part.

APPENDIX

Continue to get your Subliminal Mind to solve your problems. Do not be disheartened by failures, simply try again until you succeed. One word of warning. After receiving your answer in the early morning, you get to business, or practice, or whatever your work may be, and you may think that the answer which came to you as a flash of inspiration must be a mistake, so opposed does it appear to ordinary worldly wisdom. Be not deceived, what you have received by inspiration is the sublimest wisdom, and the so-called "wisdom" which now seeks to reverse the decision, will, if followed, lead you to confusion and disaster. Infinite wisdom always appears to be foolishness to finite man. Continue to hold a vision of glorious health and eternal youthfulness ever before your mental eyes. Also deny sickness and affirm health without ceasing, not in a strained way, but with confidence and conviction.

PART VII

TO the ordinary "man in the street" a thought is an "airy nothing "–a mere flash in the consciousness--it comes, it goes, and there is an end to it. To the student of Mind however, thought is known to be the power that is greater than any other power--a force that controls all other forces. An American writer speaking of Universal Mind says:

> "It thinks, and Suns spring into shape;
> It wills, and Worlds disintegrate;
> It loves and Souls are born."

It will thus be seen that thought is the origin of the visible Universe. All that we see around us is the result of thought. We may even go further, and say that all the invisible forces, which keep the wonderful machinery of the Universe working perfectly and smoothly, are but the thought-energies of the same Universal Mind.

As in the macrocosm so is it in the microcosm; the subliminal mind of man is the same in essence as the Universal Mind of the Universe; the difference is not one of kind but of degree.

In our world, our circumstances, our life, our bodies, we stand supreme, or rather we have within us the power, which properly directed, can make us supreme. This power is "Thought." Thought is so subtle, so elusive, that it has by the majority of men, been considered impossible of control, but the greatest philosophers, seers and leaders in the World's history have known differently. All that they achieved, they accomplished through the power of thought; and this was possible because they had learned the art of thought control. "What man has done, man can do." This was never so true as it is today, because the science of Mind is now being spread abroad, and that it is possible for quite ordinary people to learn how to control their thoughts, is now known to be a scientific possibility.

Dr. Abrams in his epoch-making book entitled "New Concepts in Diagnosis and Treatment; The Practical Application of the Electrotonic Theory in the Interpretation and Treatment of Disease," describes how he has discovered the energy of thought and measured it by means of an instrument called the Bio-dynamometer.

With one subject in a room with closed doors, and another subject, in another room, forty or more feet away, it was found that one subject could affect the other by a definite exercise of thought. Anger and emotion yielded an energy which produced an effect at a distance of eighty feet. Dr. Abrams also found that there arts three great energy centers in the human body, the right and left side of the brain, called by him the right and left psychomotor areas; and the finger tips. When the brain is actively engaged in thought there is an increase in the discharge of energy from the psychomotor areas, and also from the finger tips.

It was also found that ordinary people discharged energy from one psychomotor area only, but a great thinker discharged energy from both. The amount of energy discharged in this way can be gauged by the fact that Edward Markham, the poet, discharged energy from his left psychomotor area alone equal to a resistance of sixty ohms. As the energy discharged from a giant magnet with a lifting capacity of 400 lbs. to the square inch is only thirty-two ohms, we can form some idea of the immense power of thought which man possesses.

The flow of energy from the finger tips is also suggestive. In all ages the laying on of hands has been recognized as a healing act, now it is proved by scientific means to have been simply the power or energy of thought.

You will therefore see that "thought" so far from being "an airy nothing" or a mere flash in the consciousness is a wonderful and potent force, the most wonderful and potent force of which we know.

A man is a small individualized part of the Universal Mind, alike in essence but infinitely less in degree. Just as the Universal Mind finds expression through all the Universe, so does man when awake to his own interior powers, express himself by the power of his thought, through his body, his work, his circumstances and his life. Thus far can he go and no farther. In himself he is an epitome of the Universe, outside of the miniature Universe he has no jurisdiction. By this I mean that man has the power to do what he likes with his own life, but he has no right to dominate other people or to interfere with their lives.

I mention this because there is a pernicious practice being taught today. It is known as "mind domination." People are being taught that by using what is called the "hypnotic gaze," by telepathy and hetero-suggestion they can dominate other people. It is quite true; it can be done and is being done. This is precisely the same method as that practiced by certain criminals in America. By this method people are being deprived of money and property--they sign documents they do not wish to sign, simply because they are compelled to do so by "mind domination."

No one is to be safe from these misguided people. While you sit in a public room or theater somebody may be behind you concentrating his "hypnotic gaze" upon the back of your neck. When you receive a visit from a traveling salesman he may be working some of his mind dominating black art upon you in order to coerce you into acting against your better judgment, simply and solely that he may reap a temporary benefit.

This sort of thing is not only being practiced, but is being taught, both in this country and America.

I mention this in order to put you on your guard against such practices; first, so that you can avoid being hypnotized by these people, and second, that you should never under any circumstances use your mind forces in order to dominate other people. Whoever prostitutes his mental powers in this way is hurrying to disaster. To so misuse the tremendous powers of the mind is to destroy oneself, body and soul. All who sink to these practices are deliberately creating for themselves an inferno of trouble. The powers of the mind are like electricity; for the latter, if used according to certain laws, produces beneficial results; if used in opposition to these laws, it burns, maims, and destroys. So it is with the powers of the Mind, used aright they lead to success, happiness and all accomplishment; if used wrongly they grind to powder.

Both Hypnotism and Mind Domination are being so largely used and taught that it is advisable to always work against them. These are really a revival of the "Black Magic" of bygone days. Sorcery, witchcraft, necromancy, thaumaturgy, they are all the practice of the same power, and all who use them bring destruction upon their own heads. Sorcery, black magic, or hypnotism, or whatever you like to call it, is accomplished by the lower mind of man. The higher self, the perfect mental or spiritual creature, the real Ego, has nothing to do with it. This is why hypnotic healing is always harmful. If a person is healed by hypnotic suggestion in about three months' time either the same disease will reappear, or a new and worse disease will manifest itself. But healing done by the higher perfect mind, that is one with, and forms part of, the Universal Infinite Mind, that is in turn one and part of the Infinite Principle of Good, such healing is permanent and can have no relapse.

By this we see that the higher mind is infinitely more powerful than the lower. Therefore Hypnotism and Mind Domination can be overcome and guarded against by the use of the higher Mental Powers.

To work against Hypnotism, it is necessary not only to live as much as possible in the atmosphere of your perfect World of Mind, but also to deny the power of Hypnotism to affirm the perfect power of the perfect Universal Mind of which you, your higher self, form a part. If you work in this way you will make yourself proof against all Hypnotism, Sorcery, Witchcraft and Malpractice of every kind.

The Law which keeps the Universe running so smoothly is the law of Attraction. It is this law that brought it together; it is this law that keeps it from falling apart.

Those who practice Mind domination are acting in direct opposition to this immutable law. They are trying to do by force that which should be accomplished by attraction, therefore they are encompassing their own mental, moral and physical disintegration.

All the Universe, in all its planes, is ruled by this law; in the Spiritual World it is called the Law of Love; in the Mental World the Law of Attraction; in the Material World it is known as the Law of Affinity. They all mean the same--in essence they are the same.

Just as the electrons are called together in the invisible aether, thus to form an atom so, in turn, are atoms brought together, and by vibrating at different rates of speed, create what we call form. Thus is matter (so-called) built up into all the beautiful forms we see, simply by the Law of Attraction.

It is this law that holds all matter together. If it failed, rocks would fly asunder and all things would disintegrate, because the power that attracted one atom to another would have ceased to operate.

It is the same in the Mental World, everything works according to this same law. It is because "like creates like" and "like attracts like" that it is possible to revolutionize our lives by the power of thought. "Thoughts," said Prentice Mulford, "are things." "Thoughts," says T. Sharper Knowlson, "so far from being mere brain flashes, are, judging solely from their effects, real entities, apparently composed of spiritual substance, the nature of which is outside the range of discovery of our present faculties." "Thought," says Levy, "is not an event which dies in a world ethereal, supersensible, imperceptible; it has continually its likeness and repercussion in our organism." "Thought is not," says Ralph Waldo Trine, "as is many times supposed, a mere indefinite abstraction, or something of a like nature. It is, on the contrary, a vital, living force, the most vital, subtle and irresistible force in the Universe."

In our very laboratory experiments we are demonstrating the great fact that thoughts are forces. They have form, and quality, and substance, and power, and we are beginning to find that there is what we may term a science of thought.

We are beginning to find also that through the instrumentality of our thought forces we have creative power in reality. Many more authorities could be quoted, but these will suffice to show that thoughts are just as much "things" as town halls or mountains are "things." It is a great mistake to imagine that because you can see a thing with your physical eyes, feel it with your hands, or hit it with a hammer, that it is for that reason more real than something you can neither see nor feel. On the contrary the "Unseen" is vastly more powerful, lasting and forceful than anything you can see with your physical eyes. What you see with your eyes is only the effect of greater causes which are invisible.

"Everything exists in the unseen before it is manifested in the seen, and in this sense it is true that the unseen things are real, while the things that are seen are the unreal. The unseen things are cause; the seen things are effect. The unseen things are eternal; the seen things are the changing, the transient."

Thoughts then are "entities," are "things," are "forces," are vital subtle "powers." They, like everything else, and every other force in the universe, are subject to law. This law is the Law of Attraction.

Whatever thoughts you think will attract to you thoughts of a similar nature. According as you create good or bad thoughts, so do you determine whether your life shall be blessed or cursed. If you think a good thought and dwell upon it, and, as it were, nourish it with your meditations, it will not only bless and enrich your life, but will attract hosts of other thoughts of equal power and beauty, which will hasten to minister to you. Thus, if you think "Success" thoughts, and affirm them, and cling to them in the face of apparent defeat and failure, you will attract to yourself such a wave of powerful, upbuilding and inspiring thoughts that you will be lifted right over your difficulty and carried, as by invisible forces, along the path of accomplishment.

On the other hand, it is equally true that if you think a weak thought, a low thought, a vile thought, or a thought of failure, there will be attracted to you a host of thoughts of like character, which by their nature will curse you and drag you down. "Unto him that hath shall be given, and from him that hath not shall be taken away that which he hath" is simply the working of the Law of Attraction. Think "Success" and thousands of invisible forces will fly to your aid. Think "failure" and innumerable forces will help to make your failure even more complete.

If thought is the "greatest power of all powers," "the most vital, subtle and irresistible force in the universe," and if your thoughts have the power to attract other thoughts of a like character, then the choice of your thoughts is the 'nose important act of your life.

By choosing your thoughts you choose either success or failure, happiness or misery, health or disease, hope or despair. Says one of deep insight into the nature of things: "The things that we see, are but a very small fraction of the things that are. The real, vital forces at work in our own lives, and in the world about us, are not seen by the ordinary physical eye. Yet they are the causes of which all things we see are merely the effects. Thoughts are forces; like builds like, and like attract like. For one to govern his thinking then is to determine his life."

Therefore do not believe anyone who wants to teach you how to "overcome" other people, and to dominate them either by "will-power" or by Hypnotism. If you seek to get the better of other people and to influence them by mine domination, you are charging full tilt against the Law of the Universe, and this can only lead to the most disastrous results.

The "hypnotic gaze" and "suggestion" can never bring you success; it may bring a temporary, fleeting advantage, but this will be followed by disaster either in your business or profession, your body, your life, or your home.

By the right use of your thought-forces you can make yourself a magnet and attract to yourself all that you deserve. We each get what he or she deserves. As we improve the quality of our thoughts, so do we become deserving of better results; as we become deserving of better results, so do better things flow to us by the operation of Universal Law.

By the use of carefully graded denials and affirmations, we break the power of evil thought-habit, and in its place create a new mental attitude, hopeful, strong, cheerful, successful, confident, an attitude of mind that knows not failure, can never be discouraged; that stands firm and unafraid amid the changing scenes of life; an attitude of mind that overcomes, conquers and achieves. An attitude of mind that lives in a sea of positive, helpful, stimulating thoughts, that are the products of the best minds of all ages.

Thus it all comes down to this. It is by the use of denials and affirmations, and by persevering in their use, that the life can be changed, circumstances altered, and ambitious realized.

By denials and affirmations we can direct our thought-stream into the right channel; by denials and affirmations we can impress upon our sub-conscious mind thoughts which, becoming translated into actions, lead to success and all accomplishment. By denials and affirmations we can break down the force of evil habit, and in its place install habits that ennoble and enrich our lives. By denials and affirmations we can build up our characters, changing what was weak and vacillating into that which is powerful and stable. By denials and affirmations we can concentrate our consciousness upon thoughts of Power, Success and Courage and these, in turn, will attract to us multitudes of other thoughts of a similar nature. Do you realize, dear Reader, the extent of the wonderful power that you hold in your hands?

Make denials and affirmations to suit your particular needs. Whatever you desire to do, affirm beforehand that you can do it, and that you will do it when the time for doing comes. Whatever disagreeable or difficult duty lies before you, deny failure, and affirm beforehand that you can and will do it, that already in your Mental World it is accomplished; then visualize yourself doing the thing calmly and without effort. Mentally see yourself dealing with a difficult or unpleasant matter, with calm dignity and ease. When the time for action arrives you will succeed.

MEDITATION

Concentrate your whole attention upon the meditations. If you find your thoughts wandering through lack of concentrative power make use of the following denial and affirmation. First of all cleanse the mind by the denial of evil and calm and strengthen it by the affirmation of good. You have by so doing raised yourself into your perfect Mental World, breathing the pure air of perfect mental freedom. Now say, "Mind wandering cannot affect me. I am a perfect MIND, part of the great Universal Mind that is everywhere and works in and through everything. Therefore my mental powers are perfect. It was a mistake that made me think I could not concentrate; it was simply a delusion of the physical senses. Now I know that this could never be, because I am a perfect Mind gifted with God-like powers." Now affirm as follows: "Now I know that I can concentrate on any subject I please. My potential powers are infinite, I have only to develop them, I have only to 'try' and I must succeed." Working in this way you will develop tremendous powers of Concentration.

MEDITATION VII

I send out my thoughts to all mankind and say: "Dear everybody, I love you." Like the beams of a searchlight my mental vision sweeps over all the continents and islands of the world, and visualizes all peoples, sending out to them a great beam of Love and Blessedness. Then it takes in all sky and sun and earth and sea, and the sweet breath of heaven. It embraces all animals and flowers and loveliness, it sweeps through a thousand sunsets and a million dew-washed fragrant dawns back to the one Source of all life--again affirming, "I love you, I love you." Then into my heart flows a great wave of divinest peace, a great inrush of the accumulated love-force of the invisible Universe, I become submerged in a sea of Infinite Blessedness. Thus in blessing others do I help to make the world a little better, and in return I am doubly blessed. For this week's visualizing exercise take six small articles and examine them very carefully one at a time. For instance, if one article is a lead pencil, look at it and see in what respects it differs from other lead pencils. You notice its color; its shape, either round, hexagon or oval; its point, well sharpened or otherwise; the maker's name and trade-mark; what kind of lead, either BB, B or JIB; the name of the pencil itself; its condition, scratches on the surface of the polish; all these and many other points should be minutely noticed. Examine each article in turn and just as minutely. When you have examined them all, shut your eyes and visualize each article, and see every point and peculiarity in your mind's eye, just as you did with your physical sight. Change the articles for new ones from day to day.

APPENDIX

If you lack knowledge of a certain subject and desire to gain this knowledge, then tell your subliminal mind what it is that you require; it will then either supply direct the knowledge that you need or bring to your notice the very book or course of lessons that you require. Also in solving your problems your subliminal mind may bring a sentence to your notice, which, directly you read it, tells you that it is the answer to your riddle. The more you can quieten the senses and the objective mind and rely upon your subliminal mind the greater will be your wisdom and understanding. In the letter I have sent you this week I speak of visualizing and affirming the success that you desire to demonstrate, fn the same way hold the picture of perfect health ever before your mind. Let it be a constant inspiration and source of radiant joy.

PART VIII

THERE has been a lot of nonsense written and spoken about the Law of Attraction. People have been solemnly taught that all they need to do is to adopt a certain mental attitude, think thoughts of success and abundance, and then to sit and wait for abundance of all good things to drop from the skies at their feet. The folly of it is seen when we find that these teachers of "abundance" and "opulence" have themselves to work for a living, by teaching the very thing which, if true, would save them from all necessity of working.

Supposing it were true, then what is possible for one would be possible for all, and if all adopted this method of getting a living then who would till the soil or make our clothes? Would everything we need. come from the skies?

Even if these were true and man could draw all that he needed by the power of thought from the blue vault of heaven, then no one would have anything to do, life would become stagnant, and the race would perish from inaction.

Life is action, and if a man ceases to work he at once begins to disintegrate and soon requires six feet of earth wherein to cover his bones. When business men retire they quickly die, and those who, being born with riches have no necessity to work for a living, have to find work and interest of some sort in order to prevent themselves from mental and physical decay.

There is no such thing as getting something for nothing. The principle of the "square deal" runs right through life and the Universe. A business man who tries to get something for nothing, who, in other words, fails to give value for money, finally finds himself without a customer. Those who try to evade this law by creating trusts and combines will find that their ill gotten gains will be confiscated by a power greater than themselves. The "square deal," reasonable profits, fair wages, honest straight-forward business integrity, all these will succeed and continue to succeed, as long as there remain people to do business with; but the "ring" or "combine" or "trust," squeezing its swollen, dishonest profits out of the life and blood of the common people, can only do business so long as the community allows them to. All who read history know what has been the fate of tyrants in the past, and there is no reason for believing that the profiteers and extortioners of the present day will fare any better.

Even if, however, a man can filch a fortune by unfair means, i.e., by not giving good value for money, by extortion or profiteering, he will lose in one direction exactly in proportion to that which he gains in another. Let him make a fortune by sharp practice; let him snap his fingers and sneer at integrity and honor and universal law; let him rejoice at what he has done; let him think himself a fine, clever fellow; nevertheless nemesis awaits him. He will lose in love, peace of mind, happiness and health in exact proportion to his dishonest gain. He makes money, granted, but he loses that which money cannot buy. The writer has known men to be happy until they became wealthy, then they became of all men the most miserable. He has known them to be healthy while they were comparatively poor, and full of sickness and trouble when they became passing rich. There is a Law of Compensation running through life and the Universe and you cannot avoid it. If you are to succeed you must work and accomplish; if you are to receive the riches of the world you must give of your best in exchange.

"Then give to the world the best you have, And the best will come back to you."

This is where the Law of Attraction operates, not by your sitting still and expecting the impossible to happen, but by the giving in faith and confidence of your best efforts to the World. By calling upon your hidden powers, and by creating powerful thoughts, you attract to yourself armies of thoughts of a similar kind, which passing into your subconscious mind are translated into actions of the highest type, the type that glories in achievement, and that wins Success. Thus if you give your best to the world, then in the form of a rich and abundant success "the best will come back to you."

These people who expect to be successful without working for it, take, many of them, great comfort from John Burrough's famous poem, the first verse of which is as follows:

"Serene, I fold my hands and wait,
Nor care for wind, or tide, or sea;
I rave no more 'gainst Time or Fate,
For lo! my own shall come to me."

Never was a sublime truth more perfectly expressed, but its meaning is the exact opposite to that which the "no work" people attach to it. It does not mean that we can literally sit and "think," without effort, good things into our lap. Instead, it describes the mental attitude of the man of faith--the man who believes he can succeed. Having adjusted his mind to the correct attitude, he is serene and calm, knowing that his efforts in the objective world of effort will be successful, owing to his mental world being in tune with all the higher cosmic forces. These words therefore represent the mental attitude of a well poised, confident man, and have no connection with his physical life. Such a man owing to his mind being at peace, is always capable of the best and highest effort. It is those whose minds are at rest who work the best. Therefore those who think that they can become successful without translating their thoughts into actions, are deluding themselves.

Note the last line of the verse, "For lo! my own shall come to me." What is meant by "my own"? Obviously your own can only be that to which you are entitled, therefore "your own" can only be that which you have earned, are earning, or are going to earn,. by service to others. In other words, you have given, are giving, or will give, your best to the world, and "your own" will be the best that comes back to you through the operation of the Law of Compensation.

The principle of 'the square deal" runs through all life and the universe. Should an artist conceive a picture and be content that it remain in his mind, can he rightly expect payment for his creation? Would it be right if payment were made to him for a picture that existed only in his imaginative mind? No, because he has not rendered any service to his fellows, he has not given value for money. Let him therefore put his picture on canvas and thus bring joy and refreshment to many, and for his service payment will be made, and the greater his conception the greater will be the reward.

Again, an engineer conceives a bridge. Shall he be deserving of payment if he keeps it in his mind? No, let him transfer his mental image to paper and translate his drawings into actual steel and stone construction, and he will become a blessing to thousands. Then will he be worthy of the greatest rewards. Life demands of us a square deal, a fair exchange. If we are to receive we must give. If we give we shall receive. Do not believe for one moment that chicanery, or sharp practice, or under-hand dealing, or hiding up faults, or taking advantage of other people's ignorance or weaknesses is going to lead to success, because it will not, and cannot. I have known plenty of men splendidly equipped for the battle of life, "brainy," resourceful, capable, and not lacking in courage, yet they have not succeeded, simply because they were not "straight." They were clever and plausible and could always do well at first interviews, but they could never keep their clients or customers because they failed to give honest service in exchange for honest money.

This world is crying aloud for honest, straightforward and sincere lawyers, doctors, business men, politicians, preachers and teachers. It calls for men of integrity, men who live their lives according to a principle instead of being mere opportunists; for men who love honor and truth, for men who believe in the principle of the square deal. The world wants men who will give of their very best, and upon such is willing to pour out its treasures in rich profusion. Principle and sincerity are more than ever needed today. Men who can be trusted, men on whom a nation, a world, can rely.

No great success is, or ever can be, possible without the quality of sincerity; no great achievement was ever won except by those to whom honor and principle were as the very breath of life. Look at the lives of all the truly great and successful ones that have ever lived, and we can only find sincerity of purpose--a giving of their very best service to the world. The extent of their sincerity was the measure of their greatness. They gave of their best, and greatness and immortality was their reward.

You may not seek greatness, you may not desire to become an "immortal"; your ideas of success may be but an increase of salary, a moderate fortune, or a well paid position in your calling or profession. To be a great writer or politician or poet or philosopher or leader of men; to be one great enough in character to carve your name on the history of your time; all these may not interest you in the slightest degree or, on the other hand, they may, but whatever your ambition may be, low or high, mean or great, your can only realize it if you are sincere.

To win success of any kind you must be sincere, you must give of your very best, you must somehow find expression for that which is within you.

As you come into conscious realization of the powers within you, you will have more to express. Therefore "your best" will be constantly getting better, with the consequence that your reward will be greater. In other words, as you develop "within," as you build up in the "unseen," so in like manner will your power to achieve be manifested in your life, and success and prosperity be attracted to you. All this is dependent upon your giving freely. If you give grudgingly you will receive but a scanty reward; if you give fully and freely of the best that is within you you will reap a rich and abundant harvest.

Give the best that is within you. How can I find words with which to express all that I mean? Give your best thoughts, hold nothing back; give your most faithful service, do not spare yourself, for all the cosmic forces are yours; give to the utmost of all the powers, the forces, the emotions, the inspirations that are within you; do this, and you will never lack. The universe is not run by caprice or chance, everything is according to Law. The Law of Compensation is immutable, it can never be evaded. "Whatsoever ye mete shall be measured to you again." These are scientific facts.

Thus do we hold our lives and destinies in our own hands. We can give our best to the world--our best in service, in love, in devotion, in honesty, in faithfulness, in inspiration, in beauty--our best in all that we do or attempt to do; and back to us will come unerringly the highest good, the greatest joy, the best that life can offer. Or on the other hand we may give poor service, try to get what we do not deserve, endeavor by slimness, trickiness and sharp practice to snatch an advantage at the expense of others, and in return we shall reap a harvest of trouble, disappointment, unhappiness and failure.

"Then give to the world the best you have, And the best will come back to you."

No longer can you offer the world the more or less imperfect service which has hitherto been the best that you could offer. Now are you entering into the fulness and glory of the vast powers of your subliminal mind, now are you controlling an ever-growing stream of creative thoughts; now are all these inward forces being translated into action, and that action can only be better service, better work, higher accomplishment, more abundant success than ever you have known before.

Let imperfect work belong only to the past; the badly scrubbed doorstep, the mediocre poem, the commonplace picture, the half-hearted service in parliament; time-serving, men pleasing, instead of working for a grand ideal; let it all go, it belongs to yesterday and yesterday is dead. It belongs to the imperfect past. Now you live in a more perfect present, and press on to a still more perfect future.

Mistakes and shortcomings of the past shall have no more dominion over you; in your bands is the key which opens up the way to all freedom and accomplishment.

From now onward the new and wonderful life within you will well up with ever-increasing power and find expression in better work, in tasks more perfectly performed, in service more generously given, in more complete self-control.

Leave the past and its failures; you have nothing to do either with it or them; today is yours and the future shall be according as you build today.

This week's affirmation is:

I GIVE TO THE, WORLD THE BEST I HAVE,
ND THE BEST COMES BACK TO ME.

Then visualize yourself giving the very highest and best service of which you are capable and then picture the highest good coming back to you in return. Make this mental picture very real; it will have a great effect for good in your life. As a visualizing exercise take a flower and picture its "growth" backwards from the full bloom right back to the planted seed. Actually "see" the whole process.

MEDITATION

There is no need for me to anxiously snatch and grab, to hoard and scrape, to cheat and squeeze my fellow men. I do not have to run after success and fortune; instead, they kneel down at my feet and pay me homage. I need stoop to no subterfuges, no low cunning, no doubtful methods, for everything I need is mine, all that I desire comes to me, by the operation of Natural Law. I realize now that I am one with, and form a part of, the Infinite Mind. I realize that the Infinite Mind is "everything there is," and that everything there is is Infinite Mind. Therefore as I am a part of the Infinite Mind I too am all things and all things are in me.

Therefore everything that I can possibly require, peace of mind and health of body,. achievement of friends, love, prosperity, success, these are all mine; they hasten to minister to my eternal joy.

I am a magnet, I attract to myself only the highest good.

I am attuned only to the highest vibration of health, success, accomplishment, happiness; the lower vibrations of disease, failure, want and unhappiness can find no echo in my mind, no manifestation in my life.

I am in my inner, higher, better Self a radiant and sublime Mental Being, partaking of the nature of the Infinite Mind, of which I form a part, and in whom I live and move and have my being.

I pour out unstintedly upon my fellows my best work and efforts, my richest thoughts and emotions; I give to the World the very best that is mine. Yet the more unselfishly I give the more richly am I blest, the more abundantly are life's choicest gifts showered upon me.

APPENDIX

Give to the world the best you have, not merely your labor, your work, your earnest endeavor, but your inspiration, the very best that is in you. Not only work in the usual sense of the word, not only labor by accomplishing your daily task better than ever before, but in addition work mentally, work creatively, work along original lines. Strive to do something fresh, create something new, add something to the world's total sum of joy and happiness. This can only be done by spending your spare time, not in frivolous pleasures, but in concentration in the Silence. Still the outer mind and the senses, and then in the Silence listen to the still small voice of inspiration. Thus will you receive your message which will send you out into life with a glow of passionate desire in your heart. In this way will you conceive that invention which hitherto has eluded you. Only by this means will you be able to evolve the original idea which will make your life really successful and useful.

PART IX

MANKIND is divided into two types, positive and negative. Let me try and describe each to you.

Positive man is magnetic, attractive, courageous, happy, cheerful, healthy, energetic, is full of vitality, power and ability to succeed. He never doubts his ability to win, he never worries when things go wrong; he does not complain when things are not smooth. If he meets with a temporary set-back he becomes the more determined to succeed. He does not lay upon other people the blame of his own mistakes, but instead learns a lesson from his temporary failure which shall be a guide and beacon in all future undertakings. The positive man can always find people to believe in him and to finance his operations. He never lacks friends, for just the type of people he wants are always anxious to be his friends. Consequently men, and with them, opportunities, are always coming his way. He is an optimist, but is not foolish or blind in his optimism. He is above being petty or mean, or selfish or cruel; neither does he let hate or anger sway him or influence his life or business. He inspires confidence, compels attention, is a leader rather than a follower, and literally exudes an atmosphere of success.

A negative man is, of course, the antithesis of this type. He is fearful, given to worry, apt to look on the dark side of things. Is afraid to act too much on his own responsibility and seeks the help and advice of other people. Has difficulty in making up his mind, and when he has made it up he often changes it. He lets others pass him in the race of life and then worries because he fails to get on. He is never much of a success in life, no matter what he achieves he might have done very much better. He seldom realizes that his failures are due to his own failings but, instead, lays the blame upon other people's shoulders or ascribes his troubles to chance or ill fortune. His company is not cheerful and is not sought by other people, except one or two as miserable as himself.

All his thought and conversation are tinged with pessimism and his face, in course of time, becomes lugubrious and miserable, an accurate index of the state of mind within. He has no belief in himself. He believes in fate and the influence of outside circumstances. He is, so he says, as God made him and as environment has shaped him. If he is a failure it is, he thinks, not his fault, and if his character is not all that it might be it is due to heredity and environment.

There are, of course, infinite degrees of positiveness and also of negativeness. Therefore one may be said to be more positive or less positive according to one's stage of development, or one can be more negative or less negative according to the degree of helplessness and misery in which one may be steeped; but the essential difference is this, that whereas the positive man looks within for his power to achieve, and looks forward with confidence to the future, the negative person, on the contrary, having no confidence in himself, looks to others and outside sources for help and assistance and fears what fate may bring him. The positive man believes in himself completely and absolutely, the negative person does not; that is the great difference.

It is hardly necessary to point out that all successful people are of the positive type and all the failures belong to the negative class. If you were able to make an examination of the minds of numbers of successful men ranging from such as Lord Northcliffe, Lord Haig and Lloyd George down to the successful tradesman in your own village or suburb, you would find them to be all of this positive type. If you could examinee the minds of the leaders of the professions, the surgeons, physicians, lawyers, counsel, artists, journalists and poets, you would find them all of the positive type. On the other hand, if you get into conversation with a failure it does not matter what station in life he may belong to or what his education may have been--he may be a discredited politician, or a tramp on the road--you will find that his mind is of the negative type.

It is obvious then that he who desires to succeed must belong to the positive type. If he belongs to the wrong class how can it be remedied?

We are what we are as a result of past thinking. Our mental attitude is built up by the thoughts we habitually harbor or cultivate. Thus if we entertain positive thoughts only, and deny negative thoughts, replacing them by their opposites whenever they intrude, we gradually build up a positive attitude of mind, which means that we become positive men or women, and as such cannot fail to be successful in life. Therefore it all comes back to the old question of thought control. "For one to govern his thinking, then, is to determine his life."

Thoughts are positive if they dwell upon the following: Success, achievement, accomplishment, overcoming, conquering, mastering, prosperity, power, courage, calmness, dignity, perseverance, purposefulness, patience, wisdom, faithfulness, confidence, faith, hope, cheerfulness, love, joy, peace, health and happiness.

Thoughts are negative if they dwell upon the following: Failure, difficulty, bad luck, hard lines, I can't, fear, dread, grief, worry,

care, anxiety, loss, fate unfaithfulness, grievances, criticising others, imputing bad motives to others, hate, envy, covetousness, brooding, lust, impurity immorality, selfishness, sensuality, misery, unhappiness, disease, ill-health and death.

The former build up character of mind and health of body; they create serenity and peace. The latter break down the nervous system, produce ill health and disease, rob the life of nearly all its joys and destroy all hopes of success.

If you concentrate your thoughts upon the former for a few minutes and let the imagination play round each word, and call up in the mind just what it means, a sense of power, unlimited and all comprehensive will pervades one's being. This is the infinite powers of the subliminal mind being aroused. All these positive qualities which these words represent are within you, otherwise you could not arouse this sense of power. If, by concentrating your thoughts for a few minutes upon Success, a sense of unlimited powers of accomplishment stir within you, then you have actually within you unlimited powers of accomplishment. If, by thinking only of Joy for a few minutes, a sense of intense Joy pervades the mind, then you have simply called into activity an inexhaustible reservoir of Joy that already existed within you. You cannot call into activity that which does not exist. In the same way if you concentrate your thoughts upon a negative quality, such as misery, you will after a few minutes become gloomy and depressed, or if your mind dwells on fear, you will soon become full of dread and apprehension.

Therefore your success, health and happiness all depend upon the type of thought that you entertain. If your mind dwells upon positive thoughts only, then you become positive and by sustained action, successful. If, however, you think negative thoughts you become negative and consequently a failure.

How then shall you so control your thinking that only positive thoughts are allowed? The answer is, by eternal vigilance, constant watch and guard, and by incessant denials and affirmations. Whenever a weak or vile or unworthy thought attempts to enter your mind, deny its existence in your perfect Mental World, and affirm in its place a thought the exact opposite of the one which you have denied. For instance, the thought may come to you that you will fail at the examination for which you have shortly to sit or that a certain important interview will end disastrously for you, or that you will not be able to pay the rent next quarter day. Whatever the thought may be, if it is negative, deny it from the mind. Raise yourself into your perfect World of Mind and say "There is and can be no failure, man is a perfect mental creature, potentially all the powers of the Infinite are his, therefore he can never fail." And then affirm:

I AM SUCCESS

EVERYTHING THAT I ATTEMPT

I COMPLETELY ACCOMPLISH

I AM SUCCESS

Then visualize yourself successful in that which you have attempted, the examination passed, the interview successfully ended, the rent paid. See yourself radiant with success, feel yourself lifted up by the power within. Let the thought, "I am success," sink deeply into your sub-conscious mind; let this be projected into the space to gather unto itself thoughts of similar quality and power, which shall come back with it to minister to your joy, and you will find the negative fearing thought will flee away. Thus will you become master in your own house and captain of your soul. Thus will you be built up in character and strengthened with determination and ability to accomplish. Thus will you be enabled to go forward with joy and confidence to possess your glorious heritage.

The following affirmation used at night just as you are falling asleep will be helpful; after a few weeks it will have become unnecessary and should be discarded:

WHEN NEGATIVE THOUGHTS
ASSAIL ME I WILL DENY
THEM AND REPLACE THEM
BY THOUGHTS OF POWER.

Then visualize yourself pursuing the path of achievement which you have so often before seen in your mind's eye. Imagine that you see people trying to drag you from the path and seeking to persuade you to travel down a side turning. See yourself shake them off easily and firmly, continuing your journey to that bright vision which to you is Success.

I have said that there are varying degrees of Positiveness, just as there are degrees of Nega-tiveness. For instance, the lowest form of "success" thought is "I can succeed." A student may have all his life thought that he could not succeed. He may have thought that others might succeed because they were "clever" or had better opportunities, or were blest with "luck"; but he, poor fellow, being neither clever, lucky nor presented with opportunities, cannot succeed; he must forever be content to remain a mere hewer of wood and drawer of water. But one day, we will imagine, he reads a "Pass me on" pamphlet and reads for the first time that he has within him the power to succeed and accomplish, and like a flash he realizes his true inward powers, and cries "I can succeed."

That, of course, is the first step. Very soon he says to himself, "I will succeed," and thus finds himself on the second step, and, for some time, progresses on these lines. This is a rugged and stony path because progress depends almost entirely upon Will-power and progress by Will-power alone is exhausting and trying to a degree, but soon the student realizes that he has acquired a new or wider consciousness and says with joy and wonder, "I am success." He has now reached a higher region of the mind, he is now exercising a larger and deeper faith. He realizes for the first time that success is not something that is outside himself, or that has to be searched for or chased. He realizes that not only is success within him, but that he himself is Success. I cannot explain it further. I am dealing with a state of mind which cannot be described, but which can be experienced. When the student has attained to this stage of consciousness he can no longer fail in life. His life henceforth becomes a constant progression, a passing onwards to higher heights and more glorious achievements.

This is the reason why I have made the affirmation to read "I am Success" instead of "I will be successful." To say that you will be successful is good, but it puts off your success to a future time. To affirm that you are success or successful now is to make your success to begin here and now.

Conscientious readers will say at once: "How can I say truthfully that I am success when all the time failure enters so much into my life? I have just failed to pass an examination, and through lack of energy and perseverance have let the opportunity of a lifetime slip by; how then can I affirm myself success?" The answer is that you are success in reality. In your inward inner self you are success, because you are a mental creature and have all the elements of unbounded success inherent within you. You, your real mental inner to be. If you affirm that you are Success, and will persist and persevere with that affirmation, then in your inner self you are success, and later this will be translated into your outward life. What is created in the Unseen is later manifested in the Seen. By the affirmation "I am Success," you create Success "within";

later this finds expression in your outward life, in the form of achievement, accomplishment and material prosperity.

Therefore when a thought or suggestion of failure attempts to gain admission to the citadel of your mind, kill it by denial, and affirm in its place the "Success" formula that I have given you. Thus will the attitude of your mind be built up into a definite form. By affirming "I am Success" and by visualizing yourself as the embodiment of success. By seeing, with your mental eyes, yourself with your ambitions realized, and with all things at your feet, you will construct a concrete image in your mind, which will form a matrix, out of which will proceed the material success and accomplishment which are its visible expression.

It cannot be emphasized too much that success is not a something to be won, instead it is rather a mental state, an attitude of the mind. The mind itself has unlimited power, and mental power or thought is the power or force that is greater than all power or forces, therefore the power to accomplish all things is within us. This potent power however, cannot find expression in the life if the attitude of the mind is wrong. When the mind is naturally of the success type or is made so by training, then its intense powers become focussed into one powerful beam, which shapes and moulds the outward life, on the form of the inward pattern. There is nothing of "magic" about this, it is capable of the simplest explanation. When your mind is of this type, the impulses sent to the sub-conscious mind can only result in successful actions. As we have already seen, the sub-conscious mind is the seat of all action and contains unlimited power and energy. This power and energy only needs directing into the right channel to accomplish anything that we may desire to accomplish. When, therefore, the mind is cast in the "Success" mould, then only "success" thoughts and suggestions can go to the sub-conscious mind, and these in turn must of necessity be translated into successful actions.

The only difference between a successful type of man and an unsuccessful type, provided they are of equal energy, is one of mind--of thought. The successful man's attitude of mind is such that he generates the right kind of thought, which passing to his sub-conscious mind, is transmuted into the right type of action. The unsuccessful man, on the other hand, through his mind being of a negative type, generates the wrong kind of thought and this in turn results in the wrong type of action. This is why it is impossible to keep the "success" type of man down for any length of time. You can bankrupt him, bereave him, maim him, cast him into the gutter and jump on him, and he will come to the top again. It is impossible to keep such a man down for long, simply because his mind will not allow it. This also is why it is impossible to help a man of a negative type. The more one helps such a man the weaker and more hopeless he becomes, and the more helplessly he clings round one's neck for sustenance and support. Place him in affluent circumstances, find him work, prospects, influence, friends, place in his hands everything possible with which to aid him, and he will let it all slip through his fingers and come right down to want and penury. Therefore, success in life is the result of "success" actions, which are the result of "success" thoughts, which are the result of a "success" attitude of mind, and this is the result of the affirmation "I am success."

As the attitude of the mind alters from negative to positive there is developed what is called personal magnetism; one radiates an influence which attracts people. It is impossible to estimate the difference which this alone makes to one's prospects of success. If a man is in business for himself, what an enormous difference the drawing influence of a well-ordered mind will make to that business. His clients or customers will increase a hundredfold in number, and a better type of client or customer will gradually be attracted. Thus does success and prosperity crowd in upon the man or woman who cultivates the right type of mind. Once the right attitude of mind has been built up the trouble is not how to get business, but how to execute it. It comes crowding in so rapidly it is difficult to cope with.

Again, in all businesses difficulties appear from time to time, and although these may and do extinguish men of negative type, they cause only temporary trouble to one whose mind has been trained on "success" lines.

As explained in other parts of this course there are ways by which all difficulties can be overcome by the power of the mind, but it is only those whose minds are controlled aright who can make use of them.

Again, as the mind becomes more positive, the Will is greatly strengthened, the staying power is increased, and the powers of concentration vastly strengthened. Anyone acquainted with the difficulties and trials of establishing a business or professional practice will appreciate the value of this. Success generally comes to those with the greatest staying power. The power to "stick to it" is often the deciding factor in the struggle. Most men give up the struggle when they are just at the turning of the corner, and only a little more push and staying power would ensure success. Instead they give up through lack of "stickability" just when success is ready to crown their efforts.

Many other illustrations could be given to show how it is that success is really more an attitude or quality of the mind than something outside of us, but these will suffice. The great thing to aim at is to build up within you this "success" attitude of mind. When this is established and the habit of action well developed, there is nothing that can stay your success. Affirm that you are success now, steep yourself in the success idea, visualize yourself successful and all conquering, breathe the success atmosphere, live, dream and be success, and nothing can prevent you from being successful, because you, yourself, are success.

Do not, however, strain after success; rather realize that you yourself are "Success" and that you therefore attract to you all that you desire. Go about your duties calmly and with confidence, knowing that you are "success" and therefore must succeed. A hundred times a day, if necessary, affirm "I am success." The last thing at night, just as you fall to sleep; the first minute of your waking day, affirm it and affirm it again, always picturing yourself happy, successful and all-conquering.

The special visualizing exercise for this week is as follows: Sit upright in a quiet place and, closing your eyes, send out to all mankind the best and noblest thoughts of which you are capable, thoughts of good-will and love to everybody in all the wide world. Now feel these thoughts being projected from you in all directions, and mentally see them being sent forth like the beams of light from the light-house. See them penetrating further and further, all over your own country and then through every other country. Do this for some time and then reverse the process. Feel the thoughts coming back laden with other thoughts of a like nature. See innumerable beams of light pouring into you from all over the world. Feel yourself filled up and overflowing with the riches of all the most glorious thoughts which the world has ever known. The first part of the exercise may exhaust you, but the latter part will fill you with courage, confidence, calm, serenity and peace.

Persevere and endeavor to make this exercise as real as possible. By this exercise you enrich the world by your own noble thoughts, you lessen its pain and sorrow, and help to assuage its griefs. In return you are blessed and strengthened in a way which could never otherwise be possible. The more freely you give of your best thoughts the more bountifully you will receive.

MEDITATION

Meditate daily upon the following words of James Allen: "You say you are chained by circumstances; you cry out for better opportunities, for a wider scope, for improved physical conditions, and perhaps you inwardly curse the fate that binds you hand and foot. It is for you that I write: it is to you that I speak. Listen, and let my words burn themselves into your heart, for that which I say to you is the truth: You may bring about that improved condition in your outward life which you desire, if you will unswervingly resolve to improve your inner life. I know that pathway looks barren at its commencement (truth always does, it is only error and delusion which are at first inviting and fascinating), but if you undertake to walk it; if you perseveringly discipline your mind, eradicating your weaknesses, and allowing your soul-forces and spiritual powers to unfold themselves, you will be astonished at the magical changes which will be brought about in your inward life. As you proceed, golden opportunities will be strewn across your path, and the power and judgment to properly utilize them will spring up within you. Genial friends will come unbidden to you; sympathetic souls will be drawn to you as the needle is to the magnet, and books and all outward aids that you require will come to you unsought."

APPENDIX

Continue to deny evil, illness, sickness, disease, failure, poverty, limitation and all negative states. The more perfectly you expunge them from your mind the more blessed will your life become. Constantly affirm health, success, prosperity, freedom and all positive states, and carry a vision of them always before you.

———————

Spend as much time as possible in the Silence, for in quietness and confidence shall be your strength. Also whenever, during the day, you have to make a decision, mentally retire into the Silence and gain wisdom and inspiration from the Infinite. Thus shall you be kept from all mistakes and blunders, and your life become rich with blessing, because it is lived in obedience to Universal Law.

PART X

THERE are two great obstacles in the path to health and success. They are fear and hate. Not only do they bar the path to success, not only do they break down the health, but they also destroy all happiness and peace of mind. They are the most negative of all negative qualities and give rise to the most negative of thoughts and the most destructive emotions. They break down the fabric of the character, destroy the nervous system, and create disharmonies and disturbances which effectually keep success, health, peace of mind and happiness at a distance.

There has never been a truly great figure in the world's history that has harbored fear; on the contrary, the truly great have always been distinguished by their faith and courage. Great characters, accomplishers of great achievements, the truly successful, know full well that they can only do great deeds, or accomplish mighty purposes, to the extent that they are able to banish fear and hate from their minds and lives.

Fear is the deadly enemy of accomplishment, it paralyzes effort, destroys initiative and corrodes the mental machinery. Fear and worry go hand in hand, the one produces the other. Worry never yet succeeded in overcoming a difficulty, neither has it ever succeeded in. elucidating a problem; all it can do is to destroy health, wreck happiness and peace of mind, and make the difficulties more difficult to overcome and the problems less easy of solution.

Fear, worry, care, what a terrible trinity! How destructive they are, what numberless lives they have marred and ruined. Mental gifts, high attainments, university education, opportunities due to birth, breeding and influence, help of friends and relatives, even genius or ability almost approaching genius, all in vain, all are rendered futile, if the mind is allowed to entertain fear.

Unless fear is cast out of the life UTTERLY there can be no success. Entertain fear in your mind and you slam and bolt the door on all achievement, you sound the death knell of your hopes and ambitions.

"Fear is everywhere: fear of want, fear of starvation, fear of public opinion, fear of private opinion, fear that what we own today may not be ours tomorrow, fear of sickness, fear of death. Fear has become with millions a fixed habit. The thought is everywhere. The thought is thrown upon us from every direction. . . . To live in continual dread, continual cringing, continual fear of anything, be it loss of love, loss of money, loss of position or station, is to take the readiest means to lose what we fear we shall. "

By living in fear you not only slam the door on all progress, hut you also attract to yourself the very thing that you dread. If you dread sickness, then the fear of sickness will break down your nervous system, and this will lay you open to every kind of disease. If you fear failure in your business, then all your actions will savor of failure and your business will come to a speedy end.

Fear, worry, anxiety, dread, this dreadful negative family, are rendering miserable the lives of millions of people, and they are all the offspring of lack of faith and courage. Have faith in the omnipotence of the Power within you, and all fear will cease, and worry, care and anxiety flee away. Get right hold of the Truth that your life, your circumstances, everything that comes into your life, is the result of your thinking; that your future will be modeled exactly on how you think today. Realize that everything is in your own hands and that as you are building well today the future must and will be well. You cannot build well today and have a bad future, neither can you build badly today and reap a good future. The law is absolute, as you sow, so do you reap. Sow well today and in the days to come you will reap an abundant harvest of all good things.

Therefore get this thought right down into your being, everything is in your own hands, use your God-given faculties aright, concentrate your mind on good and positive thoughts and nothing can go wrong in the future. Think right thoughts NOW and the future can take care of itself. There is NOTHING to fear, henceforth there is nothing capricious or uncertain in your life, all is according to Eternal Law. All that you have to do is to think aright and to act aright, and all things will be added unto you.

As you bring your life, by the control of your thoughts, into harmony with the unseen higher forces, you enter into a life of peace and power. There is nothing whatever about which you need fear or worry, because you are in harmony with all the Universe. The power that maintains the stars in their places and guides the planets in their courses, is the same power that animates you. Nothing can come by chance into your life, only that which is the result of your thinking.

Now is given into your hands the power and the knowledge whereby you can control your thinking; the power and the knowledge by which you can choose those thoughts which will build up your life in beauty and strength, and ensure an harmonious future. Nothing can go wrong in your life if your thoughts are right. Right cannot produce wrong, neither can wrong produce right. Get your thoughts under control and all evil must flee away.

Therefore there can be nothing to fear, your life is in your own hands. He who is established in truth and courage need fear no evil, for evil has no power over one whose soul has cast out fear. When thoughts of fear assail you, and at all available times, make use of the following denial:

> THERE IS NOTHING IN ALL
> THE UNIVERSE THAT CAN
> MAKE ME AFRAID.

After the denial of Evil, this is the greatest denial of all. The most terrible thing in anyone's life is the belief in and thought of evil, but fear is almost as destructive. YET THERE IS NOTHING TO FEAR. There is no evil and there is nothing to fear. They only exists in our minds. While they exist in our minds they are very real and terrible, but they have no real existence apart from our minds. The only power that evil and fear, and the things feared, have, is the power that we invest them with, by our thoughts. Nothing exists apart from our minds. Everything is mind or thought, and its phenomena or manifestation.

This is proved up to the hilt by the fact that when you have, by the power of the denial, "There is no evil," and the affirmation, "There is only Infinite Good," cast the thought of, and belief in, Evil out of your mind, then you discover that there is no evil outside of human thought and that there is, and always has been, only Infinite Good. In the same way, when you by denial and affirmation have cast out fear, you discover, to your joy, that there is nothing and never has been, and never can be, anything to fear.

"There only exists that which exists in the Mind." Therefore, to cast out fear, raise yourself into your perfect World of Mind. Realizing that you, your real YOU, are a Perfect Mental Creature, radiant and divine, that you are an individualized expression of the Great Infinite Mind of the Universe, and as such, are gifted with God-like powers. Having raised yourself mentally above the world of petty strife, of limitations, and time and sense, into the Perfect World of Mind, realize that you are in harmony with and form a part of, the great Power behind the Universe, that Infinite Mind or Principle of Perfect Good, which is the guiding spirit behind all life's mysteries. Get into touch with, and realize your oneness with, this Infinite Mind of Perfect Good, and you will realize that there can be nothing to fear. You are in harmony with the Infinite Principle of Good and there is therefore nothing that can harm you or of which you need be afraid. Stand firm then, looking up, realize your one-ship with the Highest Powers, your harmony with all the Divine Forces, and use the denial unceasingly,

> "There is nothing in all the Universe that can make me afraid."

Having purged your mind of fear, next build it up and strengthen it by this affirmation:

> "I am in harmony with the Infinite Principle of Good that permeates the Universe, and against which evil has not the slightest power. Therefore I am unafraid, nothing can harm or destroy, nothing can ruffle me, or disturb my peace of mind. I am carried forward by the invisible forces of Good. All is well."

Then realize this stupendous truth, and visualize yourself standing dauntless and unafraid, serene and calm, borne up by Higher Powers. As we by the power of thought-control develop our subliminal powers, we become conscious of a new Self developing and manifesting itself within us. This is our Subliminal Self. Not only do we become increasingly conscious of the new powers within, but we also are aware of powers without us. As we develop our inward powers along correct lines, so do we come into harmony with the powers without. There are powers within and powers without, all of which will help and bless us, if we only come into line with them.

There are, of course, testing times in all lives, but to the well-trained mind these should give no cause for fear.

"It is how we bear ourselves at such times that determines our real worth and use, whether we have stamina, backbone, courage--real character--and if at such times we can stand unfaltering, uncomplaining, desirous of neither sympathy nor pity, patient but resolute, and doing today what today reveals to be done and so ready for the morrow when it comes, there can be but one outcome. The Higher Powers of all the universe stand back of such a life, they uphold it, they sustain it, they stamp it with success, they crown it with adoration and with honor." R. W. Trine in "The Wayfarer on the Open Road:"

> Therefore you have nothing to fear, so cast out fear and meet the future with joy and gladness.

The other great obstacle to health and success is hate. There can be no health or success in life for the one who hates. He who hates emits a force which rebounds back upon himself. Hate injures the one who hates far more than the one hated. Hate poisons the blood of the one who hates and tears down his nervous system. Hate is negative and destructive, love is positive and upbuilding. Hate affects adversely all the vital processes. It destroys health, wrecks happiness and turns the life into an inferno of trouble. Have you ever noticed the lives of those who indulge in hate? They are a continual round of trouble. Before they finish one brawl they find themselves engaged in another. They are at loggerheads with nearly everybody, and misfortunes seem to dog their footsteps. Misfortunes and troubles are attracted to them as a direct result of their hate. Through indulging in negative thoughts and emotions, negative conditions are produced and attracted. That is why people who hate are not always in trouble through other people's hatred, but they attract to themselves troubles and disasters which seem to have no connection with hate, but which are in reality a direct result of that condition of mind. Therefore, dear reader, if you have hatred, malice or resentment in your mind or life, pluck it out and cast it away, because you can never be successful, never be happy until you have done so.

The best way to cast out hate is to hold your mind continually in the attitude of good will to all men. If hate is to you a real difficulty, if you blaze with resentment whenever you think of a certain person who has deeply wronged you, if there wells up within you a fierce desire to get even with the object of your hatred, or at least to wish him harm, remember this, that you can never make any progress in mind and thought control you can never be successful and happy until you have forgiven your enemy. If, just as you are falling asleep you use the following combined denial and affirmation, you will find it much easier to conquer your negative failing during the next day. First of all, raise yourself into your Perfect World of Mind, deny evil and affirm Infinite Good, then say:

I FORGIVE AND FORGET ALL MY ENMITY AND ANGER, I SEND OUT THOUGHTS OF LOVE AND GOOD WILL TO ALL MANKIND.

Get your mind into this attitude and all will be well. By thinking in this way you create currents and vibrations which will bring you blessing, happiness, health, healing and success.

It may seem strange to insist upon forgiveness and love in lessons on mind training and success development, but believe me there can be no true all-round success, no happiness or harmony in life, so long as hatred, malice and uncharitableness are cherished. These are negative qualities, and success, real, lasting and true, can come only to those who overcome and cast out, root and branch, all negative thoughts, beliefs and habits. Great minds are above all such petty, mean feelings as hatred, spite and malice. It is the truly great who can best afford to be magnanimous. By regulating and controlling your thinking, by casting out fear and hate and all other negative states, you, too, can become great in mind, and noble in action.

Therefore when you make the above affirmation, visualize yourself raised above the petty cares and strifes of men, looking with a broader outlook above those who hate and squabble and disagree. There is a mental realm of peace and quietude which is far above earth's troubles. But before you can enter into it, you must first put yourself right with your fellow men. We cannot dwell there if we are not dealing fairly with the world, and giving our very best service to the cause of humanity. We cannot dwell there if we fear, we must first of all banish fear and possess our hearts with courage. We cannot dwell there if we are selfish, nor if we desire or demand for ourselves anything or state which we are not anxious that all should partake of or enjoy. But when we have put ourselves in harmony with all the higher forces, then we can rise above the things which vex and grieve the hearts of men. We can rise to a plane where absolute calm and peace continually abide.

I can hear some of my readers saying, "What has this got to do with success in life?" My answer is, "everything." It is because the majority of people are so full of worry and care that they are perplexed and anxious. It is because they are so perplexed and anxious and so wrapped up in little, petty, non-essential things, that they are never able to take the broad view and consequently can never be successful. A man or woman with a small, petty mind can never be successful; it is only those with imagination and breadth of view who can plan a successful campaign, and successfully carry it through. It is impossible for anyone to put forth his best effort if he is worried and careworn, or fearful, or full of hate. The nervous system is so weakened, the life force is so corroded, there is none of that vital, living, overpowering energy which is so necessary to success. Neither can the mind be concentrated upon the business in hand nor the problem to be solved, nor the difficulty to be overcome, if it is engaged in worry, anxiety, hate, or fear.

Therefore I say, learn to rise to that higher state of the mind where peace and calm and confidence continually abide.

The special visualizing exercise this week is as follows:

Sit yourself in a quiet place, upright in a chair, close your eyes. Now mentally send out to all the World your best service. If you are a great writer of books, see them being sent by the thousand, by rail and steamship, all over the globe. If you are a merchant or manufacturer, see your goods being dealt with in the same way. If you are an artist, see your pictures going to many lands. If you are a poet, see your poems bringing joy and peace to thousands of hearts everywhere. No matter what your occupation may be, or may be in the near future, see the effects of your service going out to all mankind. Do this for a few minutes, and then reverse the process. See money coming back to you from all over the world. Call up a clear and perfect image of money arriving by every post, in the form of drafts, cheques, money orders, or cash. See it after the envelopes are opened. See yourself counting it and piling it up. Do this for a few minutes and then dismiss that matter from your mind.

MEDITATION

There is infinite plenty and profusion in Nature for all man's wants and needs. Nature is prodigal in her provision, and would willingly clothe every son of man in plenty and abundance, if he did not create his own poverty by wrong thinking. Prosperity and abundance, in health and wealth, in beauty and happiness, in every perfect good, these are all waiting for man, did he but know it, could he but believe it. There is for every man all that the heart can wish for, but he fails to enter, because of wrong thinking into his glorious heritage. There is infinite profusion of the divinest blessings for men; they are mine now, and will come to me when I, by means of scientific thinking, have purified my thoughts and cleansed my mind. When I have got rid of hate and fear and selfishness and weakness, and have built up my mind in love and courage, unselfishness and strength, then shall I find that there is nothing in life that is too good for me, nothing in all the Universe that can be denied me. Nature withholds nothing from the man who is unafraid, and whose thoughts are in harmony with the Universal Mind, whose heart is free from hate and malice. Therefore Nature shall withhold nothing from me.

And what I affirm for myself, I desire also for all my fellow creatures, that they too may experience all the joy that I experience, and learn how to bring their lives into harmony with the Infinite Principle of Good.

APPENDIX

Continue to develop subliminal thinking. Take all your difficulties and perplexities into the Silence and let your great inner mind, drawing upon the Eternal Wisdom of all the Ages, give you the true answer that you need. Whenever you desire inspiration or original ideas, seek them in your Subliminal Mind because there alone can they be found.

PART XI

WHAT is success? To one it means one thing and to another it may mean something quite different. Some desire happiness and love above all things and could they but gain these would count themselves successful in the highest degree, even though their circumstances remained humble and comparatively poor. Some desire fame and distinction in science, their ambition is to invent, to discover or investigate, to do something that has never been done before, the only reward that they seek being the joy of accomplishment. Some again desire to be great in music, painting, in sculpture, others seek to be leaders in their chosen profession of medicine, law, preaching or politics. Others have ambitions to serve their day and generation, to give and be spent in the service of humanity. Some seek mental, and others, spiritual attainments, some again would be perfectly satisfied if they could obtain perfect health. Success in its lowest form is the acquisition of wealth, the building up of large businesses, or the earning of a large income. Although this aim is not so lofty as its predecessors, yet it is not an unworthy ambition, and if kept within bounds, will result in benefit to the community, and not too great a burden to the individual.

Whatever your ambition may be, follow it. Whatever you have a taste for, whatever it is you have a burning desire to accomplish, follow it and strive after it. It is useless to try and be successful if you are a round peg in a square hole. Before you can make your life a full and abundant success, you must find your "niche" and fill it. There is, somewhere in the world, work for you to do; work, which no one else can do as well, and which no one else can do in quite the same way. Many are the illustrations one could bring forward in support of this. Men who were anything and everything and unsuccessful in all, until at last they hit upon something which they could do a little better than anybody else and which brought them the most amazing success.

If you have an ambition, follow it, seek it, concentrate all your energies upon it. Bend and focus all the faculties of your mind towards its accomplishment. Fortunes have never been made, neither have high ideals ever been attained by half-hearted or luke-warm effort. Hit the nail of ambition on the head with all your might and strength, don't tap it like you would a tin-tack. Strive manfully, relying upon the Power within you, and sooner or later great success will be yours.

If you have not yet found your niche, seek for it: "Seek and ye shall find" is true of the mental world as it is of the spiritual. Seek, and keep on seeking, and interior illumination will show you the path, and open up the way. While searching for your niche, do not neglect your business or profession or work. Some have been foolish enough to throw up their present calling before looking for a fresh one. Needless to say this is not the course that these lessons recommend. Be like Tom Barron the poultry breeder. At one time a poor shoemaker he kept a few chickens for hobby and profit. He developed a great liking and genius for rearing chickens, but he stuck to his last. However, there came a day when his poultry rearing house became so lucrative, that after a long consultation with his wife Tom Barron decided to give up his shoe-mending and devote his whole time to poultry. Now all the world knows Tom Barron, the greatest expert in the business, the most successful rearer of egg laying strains and the richest man who ever made money out of poultry. Mix caution with your ambition, do not be headstrong, be a blend of tremendous energy, burning ambition and wholesome caution and restraint.

The way out of undesirable conditions, the path by which you will find your niche in life where your work will be an everlasting and surpassing joy, is by doing your duty in your present sphere and listening to, and obeying, THE INWARD VOICE OF WISDOM.

If you shirk duty and responsibility in order to "get on" you defeat yourself and curse your life. On the other hand, if you do your duty, however unpleasant, and shoulder, with cheerfulness, your responsibilities, no matter how heavy, affirming success, visualizing better conditions, listening to the inward voice of wisdom, you will find that sooner or later the way will be opened up before you in a wonderful manner, and you will enter into a life of great joy and usefulness.

The outward life will and must conform to the inward life, sooner or later the change must come, but only if you are calm, untroubled and serene.

In your desire to find a way out of undesirable conditions, do not be tempted to take any short cut, be guided only by the inward voice of intuition. No matter how anxious you are to change your conditions, do not persuaded to do anything that will not bear the strictest examination in the light of your highest concept of Truth.

Therefore take these "Nevers" as sign-posts and beacons to warn you from short cuts, so-called, which lead only to disaster and failure.

Never wrong anyone. Never betray a trust. Never go back on your word. Never do anything selfish. Never repudiate an agreement. Never shirk your responsibilities. Never do anything that looks mean in the light of your Perfect World of Mind.

Finally, live your life to a principle, the principle of Truth, Justice and Love.

In choosing your ambition, but more often of course it is that ambition chooses you, but whichever it is, examine it carefully and see just where it is going to lead you. Even if ambition chooses you, you still have the power to exercise restraint and to modify it according to reason. Ask yourself the question, "Am I prepared to pay the price of success?" If it is money and business success that you are going to seek, are you prepared to pay the price? Remember that men of this type live laborious days. They can never get away from their business. Many have telephones by their bedside, some have a bedroom and bathroom at their office, so that in times of stress they need not go home, but can work twenty and sometimes even twenty-two hours a day. Unless gifts with constitutions of iron such men become nervous wrecks and most of them have no enjoyment in life outside their business. Their wealth is of no use to them. In order to keep fit they have to live on the most simple fare and, as regards work and recreation, a navvy or a convict has an easy and congenial time in comparison. Their only joy is the joy of accomplishment, the glow of satisfaction at having achieved. Are you prepared to pay the price that such a success demands? If you are, go forward, and if you really believe you can succeed, and have built up your mental powers and character on the lines laid down in these lessons, you MUST succeed. Do not blame me however if you find wealth and success of this type rather a burden. The only satisfaction to be got out of it is the satisfaction of having built up a big business. I speak from experience. I went in for this type of success and in three years created, out of nothing, one of the largest businesses of its kind in the United States. But, whereas, when I had lived in a very small house and had to economize on a very tiny income, I had been very happy, when I became passing rich, the owner of a big business, and could keep one or two motor cars and other things to match, I certainly was not as happy. I would have been happier if I had modified my ambition, and had been satisfied with a smaller business, a less generous income, and had had in consequence more leisure and. opportunity for self improvement.

To all who are starting out on the road to success I offer this advice. Think well before you start, because once you have started you cannot turn back. Even if after a time you find that you have made a mistake you must keep on, because to chop and change your mental image about is to court disaster and to bring confusion into your life. When once you have put your hand to the plough you must never look back, therefore before starting make sure that you are starting on the right road. After all, the satisfying of a great ambition is not the best thing in life. If you will sacrifice part of your ambition and thus live a more normal and well-balanced life, your life will, in its broad sense, be more successful than if you sacrifice everything to the accomplishment of your desires. One can become a millionaire and be but a poor shrivelled soul in other respects. Far better is it, and I speak from experience, to aim for a broader ideal, to aspire to prosperity rather than great wealth; to desire health and happiness and peace of mind rather than to sacrifice these things at the altar of ambition.

Far better is it to build up character than a great business, to develop an insight into Nature's beauties than to own a million dollars; it is far better to enjoy good health, refreshing sleep, and a splendid appetite, than to own a kingdom and at the same time suffer from "nerves" and dyspepsia.

But whatever your ambition may be, once you have started, stick to it, do not change until your object is achieved. If you choose wealth, continue to pursue it; if greatness, concentrate all your powers on winning it, affirm its accomplishment; visualize yourself having achieved the object of your endeavors. If you will do this success will be yours.

To change about is fatal. Success is largely a matter of concentration, it is equally dependent upon staying power. Having settled upon your ambition, concentrate upon it. Let nothing turn you aside. Having mapped out your path, pursue it. No matter what opposition or difficulty you may encounter, go straight on. Remember that thought is the most powerful and wonderful power in the Universe, and that you can control your thought; therefore by controlling your thought you have perfect mastery over the most potent force of which we have any knowledge. Having perfect mastery over these most potent forces you therefore have control over your life and circumstances, and there is nothing that can prevent your ultimate success, save your own lack of faith and staying power.

Your mind actually has creative power, not in a figurative sense but in reality. All that you see with your bodily eyes is matter vibrating at different rates. The matter that you can see in this way is coarse matter. With your mind's eye you can see other matter of a finer nature. With your mind you can mold this finer matter into any pattern you please. What you create in your mind in this way, in other words, that which you visualize, if persistently held to, will form the matrix out of which will grow your outer life. The coarser particles of the outer life are shaped on the model of the pattern formed in the finer matter of the mind. This is why these lessons have persistently taught you to cast your mind in a certain attitude of thought and to visualize all that you wished to accomplish. By the use of affirmations which is thought control in its most practical form you have learned to make the most powerful use of the greatest of all powers, viz.: Thought; by visualization you put into operation a power known to the old occultists but withheld from the multitude until now. Visualization is a form of concentrated thought. It is only possible as a result of intense concentration. It is thought materialized in fine matter of mind-stuff. Therefore the more real and clear and sharply defined your mental image is, the greater your powers of concentration. The power to concentrate can be developed, and it is developed, as your power of visualizing grows. The value of concentration in business, in study, in fact, in any effort to accomplish and achieve is too well-known to need any comment. It enables you when confronted with a difficult task to get your teeth right into it and to go right to the very heart of the subject without fatigue or brain weariness. The greatest lawyers and counsel, the ablest scientists and investigators, the most successful men of affairs and business, Are those with the greatest powers of concentration. Some possess this power naturally, others can acquire it. As far as I know this course of lessons is the only serious attempt to teach this power. By the methods taught in this course you can, by the constant use of affirmations, and by persevering in the visualizing lessons, develop a degree of concentration power almost unknown in the West, approximating somewhat to the powers of certain Eastern adepts who have made concentration and mind control the study of centuries.

The writer can concentrate his whole mind and thought upon the point of a pencil for minutes at a time. Try it, and see how soon your attention wavers, how your mind wanders about the point of the pencil, but never on it. You think of other things such as concentration, of being determined to think of nothing but the point; the mind wanders off into a hundred and one things and has to be brought back again and again by an effort of the will, finally you give it up and acknowledge that is a very difficult thing to do.

When you can concentrate your whole mind and thought on the point of a needle for one minute, you will be able to accomplish anything to which you give your attention. You will have the power to take up a subject, examine it, decide upon it and then to dismiss the matter entirely from your mind. Can you estimate this power at its proper value? Instead of lying awake all night worrying over a business problem, you dismiss it from your mind and have a good night's rest, and arise in the morning with fresh energy and strength AND WITH YOUR PROBLEM SOLVED.

All your powers of concentration must be focussed on the achievement of your ambition. A clear and well defined image of what you intend to accomplish must be constantly held in the mind, AND NEVER CHANGED UNTIL THE OBJECT AIMED AT is achieved.

Visualize and affirm success, denying evil and failure, constantly and perseveringly, this is the path to success.

Remember that success is not only a matter of concentration--it is also a question of staying power. How many a promising career has been ruined by lack of perseverance and "stickability." In business and in other competitive walks of life, it is frequently the one with the longest wind who wins. The brilliant, the clever, the ones with every advantage, drop out by the way, and leave the field clear for the plodder and sticker. Therefore hold the thought "I am Success" constantly in your mind let it color all your actions, inspire all your deeds. Hold the perfect image of your success as a clear picture in your mind, persevere and hang on, and grow not weary in well doing; then whatever it is that you are aiming for will be accomplished. Be assured of this, and, again, I speak from experience, not only will your vision of success be accomplished, but it will be exceeded beyond your wildest dreams. March on, your ultimate success is as certain as the rising and setting of the sun, as sure as the tides of the eternal sea.

Make your own denials and affirmations now and henceforth, and use them as difficulties arise. Do not try to do anything without consulting your inner self and thus bringing your inward powers to action. If you feel gloomy, affirm that you are bright and cheerful; then will your gloom be chased away like mist before the morning sun. If you feel tired, affirm that you are fresh and vigorous and free from fatigue; then act accordingly, and you will find that your lethargy has flown away. If you feel care-worn, raise yourself mentally above the petty things of life, and you will find yourself dwelling on a plane, where worry and care cannot exist.

If you need guidance in the face of difficulty, when the finite mind of the senses is perplexed and at the limit of its resources, then retire into yourself and receive wisdom and guidance from the Great Within. Put the matter that is perplexing you out of your mind and dismiss every thought as it comes, until at last the mind is entirely free from thought--until it is a complete blank. When you have done this you have separated yourself entirely from the world and the life of the senses and your are in touch with the Infinite Mind of the Universe. Then will the answer come, in the still, small voice which is in every man, if he would but know it and listen for it. Whatever the answer is, act upon it, for it is the divinest wisdom.

Another method is to raise oneself mentally above the fret and fever of life, and deny evil and affirm the Infinite Good until you get a clear concept of your Perfect World of Mind. The worry or perplexity will follow you even there, but when it does, deny its existence and affirm perfect peace, perfect wisdom, perfect knowledge, perfect understanding. Affirm that man is a perfect mental creature, one with the Infinite Mind, and, therefore, in his higher self, can never be perplexed or troubled by the trivial things of the material life. Again and again the worry will come, but if you will each time deny it and affirm your perfect higher self, the possessor of all wisdom and knowledge and understanding, the thought will get weaker and weaker until it is killed altogether. Now contemplate the wonders and delights of the perfect World of Mind for a time and, after that turn immediately to, and occupy the mind with some other matter. The answer will come, the problem will be solved, and the way will be opened before you in a wonderful manner.

Another way is as follows: Just as you are going to sleep, after conquering the worry thought and rising superior to it, in your Perfect World of Mind, simply hold the problem in your mind in an expectant way, believing and affirming that in the morning the problem will be solved. When the morning arrives you will find on awaking, the solution of your perplexity, or it will come to you as you are getting up.

No matter which method you use, be sure and act upon this voice of intuition, for it is the divinest wisdom. When you get back to the hurly-burly of life, the answer will seem silly and foolish and impracticable, do not be deceived, act only upon the message which came from the Silence, do this and you will find that you have listened to the voice of the highest Wisdom. For a visualizing exercise, imagine that you have received a momentous letter from over-seas. Trace its journey back to the beginning. First the postman, the local sorting office, the mail-train, the general post-office of the large city, the mail-train from the coast, the mail-carrying steam-ship, the journey across the seas, the journey from the foreign port, by rail to your friend's home. Then see your friend sealing the letter, then see him writing it. Now look into your friend's mind and see the thought that inspired the letter.

MEDITATION

I am Success. By constant and eternal vigilance I kill by means of denials, every thought of fear, of failure, of poverty and lack, and replace them by affirmations of Success, Prosperity and Achievement. I think only of POSITIVE things, states, and emotions, and never of Negative. My mind is being constantly lifted up into a higher realm where I receive inspiration and strength. My inner Mind is one with the Universal Mind, therefore I draw upon the inexhaustible strength, energy and wisdom of the Infinite. Through thinking POSITIVE thoughts and meditating upon POSITIVE states, I attract to myself streams of thoughts and emotions of a like character, which strengthen and help me.

I grow into the likeness of that upon which I meditate, I become more Positive, I become a magnet, I draw and attract to myself all that I need. Difficulties are smoothed out, people and opportunities come to me unbidden, the way is made clear before me, and all things work together for my good. My services to the world become increasingly valuable, I get a greater and deeper insight into my work, I am inspired in such a way that I can do better work, and more work, and greater work, than ever before. Therefore I can see in my mind's eye all desirable things coming to me. All are seeking me instead of my seeking them. Friends, wealth, position, power, all are coming to me. I am a magnet. I am Success.

APPENDIX

All the good that there is in memory-training systems can be summed up in a few words. The reason some people cannot remember is because they do not pay sufficient attention. If you were making phonograph records you would have to arrange things so that a deep, sharp impression was made in the wax. If only a faint impression was made then only a faint jumble of sounds could be reproduced. It is the same with the mind if you fail to observe and to pay attention then facts, happenings, orders, etc., which should be remembered are only faintly impressed upon the mind with the unfortunate consequence that many important points and details are forgotten. The great thing to do is to observe and pay attention, to mentally impress upon your mind those which you ought to remember. A table-knife lying on the table to one person would be a knife and nothing more. If pressed for a description he might be able to say that it was either a dinner knife or a cheese knife but that would be all. A more observant person would be able to tell us that the knife was made in Sheffield and give us the name of the maker, that the blade was Firth's stainless steel, that the handle was real ivory and the tag of the knife went right through to the other end of handle. A primrose to one may be a mere yellow flower, to another it is a universe of beauty and delight. A telegraph post to one is a telegraph post only, to another it is old or new, it carries so many wires, has a crack down one side, has a certain number burned into it and shows signs of having been recently climbed by a workman with steel spikes.

Two persons may be so alike that they frequently get mistaken the one for the other, yet if you examine them carefully you will see so many points of difference you wonder why you ever thought they were alike. Their teeth are different, their ears are very dissimilar, the eyes of one are much wider apart. The hands too will show differences, the nails being of a different shape and in many other points one can find marked differences.

In order to improve one's memory one must learn to observe, to pay more attention, to examine more minutely, and to consciously impress matters that one wishes to remember upon one's mind. To. visualize whatever you desire to remember is to impress it upon your mind forever.

Not only should you learn to take more notice, to pay more attention, to observe more closely, but you should also memorize something during the day, and just as you are falling asleep at night recall what you have learned, and after repeating it over, tell your subliminal mind that you will never forget it, and you never will. This is the direct natural way of remembering, and is far better than any method which employs the Law of Association. If you follow these instructions, increasing the amount memorized each day you will develop a memory above the average.

(1) Look within for Power. Man has, in his subliminal mind, transcendental faculties, but to the multitude, these are unsuspected and midis covered. To you has been given the knowledge that has put you in touch with the Great Within. This is the key to all wisdom, knowledge, truth, understanding, achievement and power. It unlocks for you the Treasure House of the Universe, opens up to you the Wisdom of the Ages, it links you up to the Power House of the Infinite. If you are perplexed, look within, and light and leading will come, for you are one with, and form a part of, the Great Universal Mind. Have you a great task to perform? Look within, and you will find all the strength, energy, perseverance and ability that you require. No matter what your need you will find within you every quality necessary for your success.

(2) Look up. "Two men looked through prison bars. The one saw mud, the other stars." Alas that the majority of men see only mud, whereas they might, by looking up, see stars. It has been my aim to get you to look up and to keep looking up. Now let my closing words be, "look up." Hold ever before you a vision of infinite perfection and in the radiance of that vision you will find health, happiness, true success and lasting satisfaction.

With every good wish for your continued unfoldment and the greater realization of the Power that is within you.

PART XII

SAID Charles Godfrey Leyland, when over seventy years of age, "Man has within him, if he would but know it, tremendous powers or transcendental faculties of which he has never had any conception." These powers are within YOU, and by the use of affirmations and the power of mental imagery, you can arouse these vast potencies, and harness them to your service, for the enrichment of your life and the accomplishment of your ambitions.

Every act of life can be influenced by affirmations, but do not confuse yourself by employing too many at once. Seek to progress by steps, not by huge bounds which may land you anywhere but in the right place. Day by day, and step by step, is the sure road to success. Do not attempt too much, a little at a time well done is better far than a huge and ambitious scheme that may have to be abandoned. If you have a little shop do not attempt to turn it, all at once, into a huge department store. Seek first to make it by far the best small shop in the district. Make yourself very efficient in your small shop, and it will not be very long before the opportunity comes for you to take a large one, or to buy a bigger business. As you outgrow that, other opportunities for expansion will come your way, and thus will you grow from small beginnings to great things. Suppose you have a small law practice, do not try to blossom out all at once into a high class, lucrative, exclusive practice. Seek first to make yourself so exceedingly efficient in your small practice that you will be prepared for the high class practice when it comes. Affirm success and keep visualized in your mind the exact kind of success that you desire, and ways and means will in time be provided. But remember to travel step by step, to grow gradually, to develop, like a plant, on natural lines. Remember Nature is never in a hurry; all her vast works are accomplished slowly, methodically, step by step, cell by cell, but whatever she seeks to do is ultimately accomplished. So will it be with you. You have the knowledge by which you can develop your success with mathematical exactitude. All you have to do is to put the Law into action and to advance step by step. Begin with small things; when you have conquered in small things you can pass to greater, and from greater things to boundless power.

Do not expect the maximum of success at once. If you get only partial success at first, be satisfied, knowing that you will keep on improving. Even if you fail utterly you will be stronger and better for having tried. "It is the law of the reflex nerve system that whenever one does, or endeavors to do, any given thing in a certain way, a modicum of power is added whereby it is a trifle easier at the next effort, an added trifle at the next and the next, until that which is difficult and is done only with great effort in the beginning becomes easy of accomplishment--that which we do haltingly and stumblingly at first, by-and-by, so to speak, does itself, with scarcely or even without any conscious effort on our part. This is the law; it is the secret of habit forming, character building, of all attainment."

If you set out on a certain course, to accomplish a certain work, to overcome an evil habit, to repair and strengthen a weak part of your character, or whatever it may be, NEVER LEAVE OFF UNTIL YOU HAVE ACCOMPLISHED THAT WHICH YOU SET OUT TO DO. To leave off before you have conquered is to play fast and loose with your mental powers and to do them irreparable harm. Never leave off one thing and start another; instead concentrate, concentrate, concentrate upon what you have decided to achieve. Above all, live your life according to a principle. This will steady the most vacillating character. It is possible for a simple person to estimate with mathematical exactness the result of a right action, but the wisest and cleverest cannot foretell the result of an unprincipled one. The first is according to Law and produces certain results; the second, i.e., an unprincipled action, is against the Law and no one can tell where the evil effect will end.

Live your life to a principle and you will always know how to act in all cases of uncertainty. Set up as your standard the highest aspect of Truth of which you know and bring everything into line with it. When confronted with two or three courses of action and you do not know which to follow, compare each line of action with your principle, and adopt that one which is in harmony with it.

When once you have learned to live your life according to a principle, you will feel a great load lifted from your mind. For the first time there will be certainty and precision in your life and absolute peace of mind. You will have nothing to worry about because you know that your line of action will always be right, and can only bring the highest good into your life.

Never wrong any man, never take advantage of one with less knowledge that yourself, never sacrifice your principles, never give up your ideals. See that you are known for your integrity and absolute honesty, as well as for your cleverness and capacity. It may look, on the face of things, that this course of action is not going to lead to success. You see so many of your competitors making money by sharp practice, and you feel that by adopting an honest line of action you are simply putting yourself up as a target for people of less principle to shoot at. That is what it looks like, but I can assure you, speaking from experience, that the reverse is the case. It is the man of probity and honor who scores in the long run. When in business I was more successful than anyone in my line had ever been before, and I never found it necessary to be "sharp" or "over-reaching." I never practiced "salesmanship" yet I had more business than I wanted; I never went out of my way to get customers, yet they swarmed into my place from morning till night.

I once knew a theatre manager who suddenly began to live his life to a principle. Instead of covering up occasional defects in his shows as he had formerly done, he made it a principle to point them out to his customers. Many of his friends said he was a fool and prophesied his ruin and failure, but instead his business grew and flourished His friends were very surprised at his success, but they need not have been. The theatre manager was simply coming into line with eternal law, he was putting into action forces which could not fail to bring him success and prosperity. Do not misunderstand me, it is not enough to be honest or to live one's life to a high principle, but all other things being equal, it will be the man of integrity who will win in the end.

Therefore live your life to a principle, and persevere with the course which you have laid out for yourself. Be constant, be true, be faithful, be strong, be persevering, be fair to yourself, be fair to the wondrous inward powers which are seeking to find expression in your life.

Remember the law of compensation; if you are to receive the highest good in your life, you must give the world your best service.

You cannot cheat life, you must give your very best if you are to receive the best in return. It is useless to potter along and copy other people, or to do as your father did, just because he did it. There is nothing more nauseating than to see a man copying, or trying to copy, another man's success. BE ORIGINAL, BE YOURSELF. See where other men are lacking and supply what is necessary. It is the man who comes along with a fresh idea, who breaks new ground, who discovers a want which other people have never seen, who inaugurates a better service; in other words, it is the one who gets ahead with his ideas, and is the first in the field, who gets the business and makes a fortune. Therefore be original, do not copy other people. Do not be a feeble reflection of someone else; be yourself. Remember that there is something you can do better than anyone else, that no one can do it as well as you, or in precisely the same way--in other words you have personality. Therefore, develop your personality; let all your work be distinctive; make it different from that of your competitors. Let your personality be written all over your business; let there be a personal touch about everything that you do. This will distinguish both you and your business from other people and other people's businesses; this will be a reason why the public, or a large portion of it, will come to you, or will buy your goods rather than go elsewhere.

If people are to prefer your business or your professional services to those of others there must be a sufficient reason. They are not going to do this simply because you affirm that they will. The only way to get them is by supplying better goods, more perfect service, higher skill, greater probity and trustworthiness.

Another great factor in winning success is the mental attitude of cheerfulness and brightness. People are attracted to the cheerful, optimistic person, and repelled by one who is gloomy and pessimistic. Be cheerful and bright under all circumstances and this alone will be worth a king's ransom to you. These qualities alone will bring you in more money every year than most people get by hard work, to say nothing of the joy and cheeriness which this attitude of mind will attract to you. By your brightness, cheerfulness, and optimism, by your appearance and personality, you will create a good impression wherever you go. I mention appearance advisedly, because the face becomes in time an index of the soul. Just as vice becomes deeply marked on the faces of its devotees, so does the face of one whose mind and thoughts are directed into right channels, reflect the calm and peace and courage of the mind within. As time goes on the face as well as the attitude and carriage of the body alter considerably, and this makes one more attractive; thus do you attract success, because if you attract to yourself people of the right kind they bring potential success with them.

One word of warning and it is this: exercise a wise business prudence. Do not, just because you feel within you the fluttering of a new and wondrous power, rush thoughtlessly into business speculation, which may either ruin you or seriously jeopardize your business. Be prudent, be wise, be not carried away by your enthusiasm; instead, go slowly and feel your way, as it were, step by step. Be sure and steady; do not risk failure for the sake of getting on more quickly.

Keep your expenditure within your income. He is a happy man who spends less than he earns. The troubles of many families are due to their expenditure being in excess of their income. This leads them into endless difficulties and cares.

Success is no success that does not extend to the home. By scientific right thinking, happiness, peace and harmony can be made to reign supreme where formerly there were misunderstandings, friction, bickerings and great unhappiness; while ever-increasing health will manifest, instead of intermittent sickness.

Cleanse your own heart and mind by denials, build up your own character by affirmations, calm your own spirit by dwelling in the perfect purity of the transcendental World of Mind, and you will find, strange though it may seem, that everybody else in your household will get more lovable, and helpful, and restful, in their attitude toward you.

Remember to "reverse" every undesirable thought, suggestion, sight, or impression that comes to you. Deny them each and all in your perfect World of Mind, and affirm their opposite. For instance, two members of your family may be getting angry with one another and the air becomes electric. Immediately raise yourself into your higher World of Mind and say: Perfect man is never angry. He is a perfect mental creature dwelling in the pure atmosphere of the Infinite Mind and can never get angry"; then affirm: "Man is love, perfect love; he dwells in the atmosphere of the Infinite Love." If by so doing you get a clear concept of that perfect World of Mind, which IS perfect, and IS real, and IS permanent, and a clear realization of the perfect Love of this Perfect World, then the quarreling ones will cease to quarrel, will love one another instead, and ever afterwards will quarrel less.

Remember the three great Laws: (1) The Law of Love and Attraction. "Give love, and love to YOUR heart will flow, a strength in your utmost need." (2) The Law of Compensation. "Then give to the World the best you have, and the best will come back to you." (3) The Law of Absolute Justice. "For with what measure ye mete, it shall be measured to you again." Therefore the ability to win the highest and truest success, to draw to yourself the greatest happiness, to create in your life the highest good, all depend upon giving. The mistaken idea of the animal mind that, to be happy and successful, one must seize and grab, is entirely false, and leads to bitter disappointment. The voice of Wisdom that is heard in the "Silence" tells us that only as we give do we receive. That if we give of our best--our best thoughts, emotions, service, love--then the best will come back to us in the exact proportion, no more, no less.

Again let me emphasize the necessity for "stickability" and perseverance. Keep at it, never know failure, let this word be expurged from your vocabulary. It is the man with the greatest staying power who wins through hard times.

Again, possess your soul in courage. Remember that if you use your inward mental powers aright, and bring your business and your life and your conduct into harmony with the Law, you can never fail. Great are the possibilities of your life, because great, beyond all human ken, is the Infinite Power within you. You have nothing to be afraid of. Big corporations cannot smash you. You fan always beat them by personal service, by individuality and originality. By straight dealing, by integrity, by honesty combined with efficiency, and businesslike procedure, you can make for yourself an enduring reputation. When faced by problems, difficulties and perplexities, you can at once raise yourself into your perfect World of Mind, and realize that you, your real self, can never be perplexed, because being one with the Universal Mind all wisdom is yours. You know that in the "Silence," having hushed the loud voices of the surface, material mind, you can hear the still small voice of intuition, of infinite wisdom. For you, having learnt how to raise yourself above the life of the senses, to the perfect World of Mind, there is wisdom, understanding and illumination; there can be no perplexity or worry, only infinite calm and peace.

By being calm and unflurried, by dwelling in an atmosphere of peace, you can preserve your nervous system and your health, tine while your "sharp practice" competitor is tearing his nerves to pieces and breaking down his constitution.

Above all, remember to deny every thought, sight, influence and suggestion that is evil, or pessimistic, or material, or fearing, or selfish, and create in its place its exact opposite. Deny evil constantly, and affirm Infinite Good, deny fear just as frequently and earnestly, and affirm confidence and courage; do this persistently and you will transform your life.

Now that you have finished the lessons do not lay them lightly aside, and forget them. This Course is not for three months merely, it is for your life. You have gone diligently through the Course and probably think that you have mastered it, but it is highly improbable that you have. If you w ill now begin again and start with Lesson 1 and work steadily through the Course you will find fresh light and understanding, and many hidden and deeper meanings, unsuspected before, will come to light. Study the lessons and practice their teachings for the rest of your life. Do not expect immediate results. The effects of thought are slow in manifesting. It is my experience that what we think today becomes manifest in about two year's time. By that I do not mean that by affirming certain qualities I do not immediately begin to develop these qualities, because I do right from the first affirmation. What I do mean is this, that suppose I want to demonstrate a big business, a large practice, or say a house in the country all bought and paid for, a perfect recovery from life-long ill-health, or a greater advancement in spiritual unfoldment, then if I hold in my mind a sharply defined picture of what I want, and vitalize it by joyful emotion, and confident affirmations, and spend at least a quarter of an hour every night and morning holding this picture in my mind besides calling it up at intervals during the day, then in about two years' time what has been held in the mind will become an actual accomplished fact in my life. I may have many setbacks and disappointments but if I persevere and persist and concentrate, then whatever I desire MUST objectify in my life. Actually, of course, I have been progressing all the time towards the realization of my desire, but it is in about two years' time that tangible results usually are seen. After that one can never look back, because success attracts success and once one has "demonstrated," one becomes so full of success vibrations that success becomes the habit of one's life.

Therefore, keep on persevering, persisting. Never cease mentally to picture and affirm confidently. It is by this mental activity that you win success, it is not done by striving so much as "thinking" and visualizing. Of course one must work, but it is the mental activity that crowns the work with lasting success.

By bringing into play, as taught in these lessons, the illimitable powers of your subliminal mind, by the use of denials and affirmations, by harmonizing with Immutable Law, and by the art of visualizing, you can accomplish all that you desire. There is no height to which you cannot climb, no success that you cannot achieve, no happiness that you cannot attract into your life. All things are yours. Everything has been delivered into your hands. You can do whatever you please, you can achieve what you will, you can be all that you desire. Act according to the teachings of this course, making in future your own denials and affirmations as are required, extemporizing your own meditations, and you will have set your feet in a path that leads ever upward. Where it ends, if it ever does end, no one can say, but this I know, it is a path of joy and blessing and happiness and success; it leads to heights the grandeur of which cannot be described.

If I have helped you to take this road of scientific right-thinking, which leads to your eternal joy and satisfaction, I am rewarded above measure.

I affirm for you Success in its richest and fullest sense, and all the joys of overcoming.

The Advanced Postgraduate Lesson concentrates and condenses the whole of the teaching into one Meditation to be used night and morning. It is advanced in that it passes from the "I am" stage of personal consciousness to the "Thou Art" stage of union with the Divine Mind and Spirit. If it is in this respect too advanced for you and you seen to lose touch through it, I would advise you to modify it by using "I am" instead of "Thou Art."

It is hardly necessary to state that it is very important that every thought expressed in the meditation should be REALIZED, FELT, and, if possible, VISUALIZED. Some students find it helpful, when they affirm success, or health, to feel and realize that streams of Divine power and life are flowing into them from the One Fountain of all Life and Energy, others get the best results by a sheer realization of the infinite Perfection of the Absolute.

With every good wish for your continued progress along these lines.

The Advanced Postgraduate Lesson

THE object of this postgraduate lesson is to concentrate all the teachings of the course of lessons which you have been studying, to arrange it in such a form that you can make use of it to the greatest practical advantage day by day and at the same time raise the whole teaching to a higher plane. You have been taught denials, affirmations, visualizing and meditations, it will now be shown how to combine all these into one exercise, which if performed IN THE SPIRIT, as well as the form and the letter, every night and morning, will keep you in health, prosperity, love, joy and gladness, enabling you to draw around you invisible forces, which will shield you from all harm, danger and disaster. You will also be shown how to draw your loved ones into the same Divine influence and thus bless, protect and enrich their lives as well as your own.

At this point let me say that it is impossible for you to fail, or for the Laws of the Universe to cease to act. Neither can you fail to bring yourself into. harmony with these Laws if you conscientiously follow day by day the teaching laid down. I do not mean by this that you will IMMEDIATELY be healed of a long standing infirmity, or that you will be INSTANTANEOUSLY delivered from disharmonies and limitations in your life and circumstances, or that you can at once keep out of your family circle evils which have been present for a long time. What I do mean is this and I want you to pay special heed to what I say: Every time you turn to the Infinite Mind, the Absolute Divine Centre, God, Infinite Spirit, whatever name you prefer to use does not matter (neither does it matter if you seek Infinite Good within you, or above you), every time you get into conscious union with the Divine Spirit and in touch with the real spiritual world of perfection, and then deny the evil in your life and affirm all the Infinite Perfections of God, then definitely and with absolute certainty a portion of evil will be taken out of your life, and a corresponding amount of good will take its place. There is no chance or luck or mistake, or missing fire, or uncertainty about it, the Law is absolute and immutable and can never change or vary, neither can the Infinite Power, which is always at your service, fail to operate. The Law and Power which cause the Sun to rise each morning with all its glory, beauty, majesty and power, are the same which operate in your life and mine, and they can no more cease to operate when we, through denials and affirmations, consciously employ them, than the sun and our planet could resist the power which sustains them and the Law which guides their progress. The Law is changeless, in this are our strength and confidence. What we have to do is to harmonize with the Law, if we do this then our life will be gradually righted and our troubles smoothed out. Results always appear to be so slow in manifesting, yet when they do manifest and we look back on the comparatively short time the transmutation of evil into good has taken, we are amazed at its swiftness. When we consider to what straits wrong thinking had brought us, and the great accumulation of evil which past wrong thinking and consequent action had built up, it is amazing that ever we can overcome it in this life, and demonstrate the highest good in its place. Yet it is not only possible, it is being done every day. It is the greatest possible tribute to the intense power of scientific right thinking. I said just now that results always seem slow.

Some people have to wait years for the realization of their demands, but the building up process which results finally in the accomplishment of their desires, is going on daily and hourly, and every minute. The point I want to drive home is this: You can never fail once you understand the higher spiritual law of demand and supply and work mentally in the Silence each night and morning. You may not see results for many months but you can rest assured that the change is taking place hourly, the evil is being abstracted and replaced by good. It is not a question of doubt, uncertainty, of WHETHER you will be healed or not, or WHETHER you will be successful or fail, for no such question can arise, it is just a case of working steadily on, believing and knowing that the wonderful transformation is taking place, until the manifestation appears and the demonstration is made. Every time that you look to your Divine Source and raise yourself into the higher world of Cause, you drive out of your life a little sickness or liability to illness, a little failure, a little poverty of life or soul, a little misery or unhappiness, a little friction and trouble, some weakness of character, some blemish and imperfection, and in their place is brought in a corresponding amount of health, success, abundance, happiness, harmony, peace, strength of character, perfection of soul. The change is so slight it is not noticed for comparatively long periods but the work is constantly and surely going on. It will not, however, go on satisfactorily if the mental work done is spasmodic. It is only by regular and consistent, persistent work in the Unseen that results can be achieved. The time spent each night and morning need not be long, but the work must be regularly performed, never on any account omitted or slurred over, and one must get into touch with the Unseen. Students often write and say, "I cannot give your system the time it deserves, I am so busy." No one is too busy to do what I want them to, and in this lesson it will be seen that a few minutes spent in the Silence night and morning will embrace the whole of my teaching in past lessons. Of course results will come more quickly if more time is devoted to this mental work in the Unseen, what I am teaching you is the minimum which will bring result. Unfortunately most people are too busy almost to live, and also if they are asked to use their mental powers considerably they get tired and discouraged, therefore my object is to make my system take up as little time as possible and yet produce the desired results. Those who can do so should for their own sake devote more time, in fact as much time as they can spare, without causing them to neglect family, social or professional duties.

No one can ever be too busy to follow this system, for what has to be done can be done while in bed, or while dressing, or undressing, or walking, although it is better to put aside a few minutes night and morning specially for the purpose, and he or she must be very busy who cannot manage to do this. An exception has to be made in the case of those who want to find God-consciousness and unfold their own divinity.

In the lessons of the Course there was a considerable amount of the "I will" and "I can" philosophy, it is now sought to introduce you to a higher plane. Incidentally it will bring you face to face with a great mystery. You will now be taught not to affirm I am this or I am that, but to affirm instead that in God or Infinite Mind are all the perfect qualities and good that you desire, or which you wish to bring into the lives of others. A life of perfect success, health, harmony, joy, love and blessedness becomes possible only when we get rid of our finite personality and lose it in the Universal Mind. You will wonder how it is possible to fill your own life with good, and also the lives of others, by affirming that it exists in the Mind of God. The answer is the greatest mystery of all. It is that the Infinite Mind of God is hidden within the self of each one of us. The great truth which has been hidden in all religions but which has never been taught to the multitude, being only revealed to initiates, is that God or Infinite Mind is within man--that God and man are one. The realization of this blinding truth comes only to those who by patient meditation gradually unfold the inner Self, until at last they get glimpses or flashes of the Universal Consciousness, which finally merge into full realization.

If you desire to probe the great mystery and to unfold your inner Self and thus find God, I can say this: If you will sit in meditation daily and seek God, you will surely find Him, not in any particular religion or creed or dogma, but in your own soul. The greatest mystics all bear the same testimony, all describe the same experiences, all speak the same language. As Dean Inge says, it is not possible to tell which religion a mystic belongs to, for their experiences are all the same. Therefore if this is the evidence of the great mystics of all ages and all religions that God is within the soul of man, then it must be true, for this is the only thing upon which all religions and philosophies agree, and it is vital and fundamental, while all the rest, all that makes one religion or philosophy different from another religion or philosophy is non-essential, is mere padding and symbol and verbiage. But the eternal truth lives on and remains unaltered. Religious belief and philosophies alter with their environment and with changes which the passing ages bring, but the eternal and glorious truth that God lives and dwells in the soul of man and IS the soul of man, this great truth lives on and will never fade.

Therefore if your desire is to pierce the great mystery and to find your own Divine Self, your Centre, the Indwelling Spirit, the Immanent God within the Soul, then you must spend much time in the Silence in communion and meditation. This sort of thing cannot be accomplished by the utilization of odd moments, for the more time you spend in meditation the greater will be the revelation and the sooner will that revelation take place.

Therefore sit in the Silence and meditate on all the wonderful attributes of God, realize the Immanence of God, how He is in everything and in your own soul, that God and you are one. In time you will get flashes of Universal Consciousness, glimpses of the blinding truth. These will in time give place to what is called "transforming union," or as some Mystics call it, "deification." After that everything else fades into insignificance.

Of great assistance in one's progress towards God-consciousness is the study, appreciation and love of beauty. To spiritually understand a simple wayside flower is to enter into the very heart of God.

The greatest attributes of God's character is Love. To meditate upon the words "God is Love" is to enter the highest wisdom. If love is the crowning glory of the Mind of God, so must it be ours, for God and man are one.

I present these thoughts for those of my students who are seeking the deepest wisdom, the greatest joy, the highest achievements of all. They are suggestions only, but if followed they will lead to results beyond present comprehension.

However, this is not the main object of this lesson. The main object is to show how to burn up the evil in your life, and bring in a continuous stream of good, but the foregoing helps us to understand what is to follow. My desire is to show you how to work in the highest possible plane and this is by realization of the Infinite Perfection of God. By so doing you will work in a realm of far higher vibration and thus will you and your life be transformed. It is by looking to and aspiring after God transcendant that you realize the power and presence of the Immanent God in your own soul, and you have only to affirm and realize that all things are in God to draw them into your own life. The system which follows brings into play all that you have already learnt, it is a combination of meditation, denial, affirmation and visualization. By using all these methods and powers in order to produce an inward realization of the Infinite Perfection and Plenty of God, and by this realization itself, there takes place a joining of forces between God transcendant and God in your soul, which burns up the evil in your life and fills it with Infinite Good. Every time that you cause this realization of Divine Power to take place, a certain amount of evil is destroyed, and good is installed in its place. Therefore there MUST come a time when the evil will have disappeared to such an extent, and good accumulated to a point, when the latter can no longer be hid but must manifest in the life.

In the lessons which you have already read I repeatedly warned you against changing your visualization, because it would bring confusion into your life. The change which I recommend now will not cause more than a temporary upset in your life. For a few days there will be a certain amount of disharmony because of the change in vibration but that will soon cease. This teaching does not contradict what you have already learnt, instead it is its consummation. You have been prepared by the lessons which have already been absorbed, for the higher lesson which is being taught now.

During the lessons you have been trying to form a clear visualization of what you hope to be and what you hope to achieve. The only alteration that is necessary is to visualize and realize the perfection of God and Heaven instead of yourself. You drop the mortal self and find God in its place. Instead of visualizing your own achievements you visualize and realize the Infinite accomplishments of Divine Mind. Working in this way you raise the whole tone of your work, you put it upon the highest possible plane. It is necessary to mention at this point, that you cannot actually visualize God but you can TRY to, the nearest approach you will ever get will be an inburst of spiritual light. When this takes place you will know that your treatment is effective. You can, however, visualize all the beauties and wonders and abundance of heaven or the perfect World of Mind and Spirit, but see this if you can as luminous with a heavenly light all its own. Here let me say that the brighter and more luminous your vision is, and the more bathed it is with spiritual light, the greater will be the results which will be achieved.

If you are seeking to demonstrate improved circumstances by visualizing and affirming, then you should keep on doing so, and raise your mental work so as to see and realize how infinite plenty. and abundance are in God. SEE wealth and prosperity proceeding like a fountain from the heart of God, showering upon you abundance beyond description. Realize that all things are God's and proceed from God, and therefore yours, because God and man are one. Remember, YOU CAN NEVER FAIL. No matter how poor one may be, nor how desperate and hopeless financial affairs may appear to be, it is impossible for you to fail in your demonstration of abundance. God is the source of everything--is everything. Everything that we need is an expression of God and proceeds from God. The great secret is this, that God withholds nothing from man for we are part of God just as a leaf is part of a tree. The tree does not withhold its nourishment from the leaf, neither does God withhold abundance from us. In fact everything is ours already and if we do not visibly possess an abundance of all good things it is because we keep good away through negative thinking and through not claiming that which is already ours.

Therefore if you will spend as much time as possible in the Silence, both night and morning, affirming and visualizing the Infinite Plenty and Abundance of God, and SEE all the profusion of God's abundance coming to you, and you realize and affirm that it all comes from God and is already yours, if you will do this regularly every night and morning, for as long a time as possible, you can never fail. Sooner or later the demonstration will be made and you will realize everything that you have visualized and affirmed. It may be two years or it may be only a few months, before you see results, but all that time the change will be taking place, the ground prepared, the material got together for the demonstration. First in the Unseen then in the Seen, this is the Law of the Universe.

I know that many of my readers will say they have souls above such sordid things but on the other hand there are those upon whom difficult circumstances, if not actual poverty, press very hardly, and they feel that the first demonstration they must make must be that of prosperity.

The visualization must be clear, the affirmation fervent and backed by strong emotion. Also affirmations should be preceded by denials of poverty and lack, these will help you realize the Infinite Abundance of the Divine Mind.

Those who wish to demonstrate abundance should follow the above programme in addition to the "treatment" described later on in this lesson.

Those who are seeking to demonstrate abundance must notary and accomplish this by their human mind or by using their mind in a hypnotic way, for if they demonstrate wealth in this way other evils will appear in the life to take the place of poverty. Instead one must look ever to God and see Infinite Abundance coming from Him. Also evil must be denied as much as possible and perfect Good affirmed in its place.

GENERAL TREATMENT

The method I myself employ and which I wish to teach you is as follows:–

First of all say earnestly, and realize the truth of what you are saying, "There is no evil, there is only Infinite Good." Now rise in spirit to God transcendent and say, "Thou art the Infinite Good, the Infinite Perfection, the Infinite Beauty and Loveliness." As you say each of these words, visualize them and realize in your own soul what they mean. Try and get a comprehensive and spiritual idea of Infinite Good all through the Universe, try and realize what Infinite Perfection is; now by your recollection of lovely flowers, and glorious sunsets and sunrises, try and understand what God's Infinite Beauty and Loveliness is. Proceed to realize in your own soul the meaning of everything that follows, spending a little time over each, so as to get the realization. "Thou art the Infinite Love (dwell especially on this), Joy, Peace and Happiness.

Thou art the Infinite Abundance and Prosperity, the Infinite Success, Achievement, Accomplishment, Persistence, Perseverance, Patience, Overcoming and Victory. Thou art the Infinite Wisdom, Knowledge, Truth, Light Understanding, Justice, Equity, Honesty and Uprightness. Thou art the sure guide of all who know Thee. Thou leadest man always in the right path, showing him step by step the way for him to travel. Thou art the great solver of all problems, man can never be perplexed or dismayed, for Thou dost solve all his problems immediately and the Divine Spirit within him tells him exactly what to do."

"Thou art the Infinite Life and Health." There is no disease, sickness, ill-health or infection. (Here deny your own weaknesses and ailments, realizing that they cannot exist in God.) "There is only Infinite Life, Health, Purity, Perfection, Loveliness, Beauty, Youthfulness, Joyousness, Happiness and Love."

This will cover every department of your life. Deny especially the troubles, habits and difficulties of your own life, and realize that they can never exist in God. This will make it easier for you to realize their positive opposites as they exist in God. It is all a question of realization, for it is only when you realize the Infinite Perfection of God, that the "treatment" becomes effective. When you get the realization you will become conscious of an inburst of spiritual light, of radiance and glory. Also you will feel lifted up in spirit in a wonderful manner. Realization is the only thing required, because the power of God is infinite and comes into operation as soon as you spiritually realize it within the soul. Therefore when you realize that there is no disease or failure in God, and that, because you are in God and form part of the life of God, there can be no disease or failure in you, these negative evils begin to vanish from your life, simply because they cannot exist where God is.

You will observe that the whole "treatment" is a meditation, therefore every time you do this you become more like God and your life more like that of heaven. Every time you "treat" in this way, you are putting away the old life and its failure, and entering further into the Infinitely perfect life of the spirit. If you make a daily habit of thus "treating" and entering more into the Divine Life, you will, as the years go by, find your life become more and more harmonious, beautiful and blessed, and more like that of heaven. At first, of course, the old troubles will persist, but in time their violence will diminish and they will come less frequently until finally they disappear altogether. Persistence and perseverance are necessary. Many times you will think you are doing no good, but if you will persist and persevere you can never fail. The results are a foregone conclusion, for you are dealing with Immutable Law and the Infinite Power of the Absolute, therefore you can never fail. Results may be delayed, owing to accumulated past wrong thinking, but they will surely come, and they will come in this life.

The results are not, however, confined to this life, for every time you "treat" in the manner shown you are building up your soul-body and your spirit-body and thus preparing yourself for the lives which have to be lived, after you have shuffled off this mortal coil. According as you build now, so will your life be when this transient passing vapour is finished. He or she is wise who builds well today.

It may be as well to say at this point that you should continue to use denials and affirmations at all times during your waking hours. They will not hinder you, instead they will speed your work and make your tasks far easier. Also they will smooth your pathway and round off life's sharp corners. You may have to live or work in a sea of irritability, yet if you will deny that these things can affect God's creatures, and affirm that all is peace and love and joy, the disturbances will quickly pass away.

It must be pointed out that the more often you raise yourself into the perfect world (heaven) and turn to Divine Mind (God) and affirm the wonders and beauties of His Character, the greater progress you will make in the new life, the higher your achievements will be, and the happier you will become.

I have shown you how to "treat" for yourself, I will now show you how to "treat" for others and cure them or be the means of their cure, of sickness of mind, body or estate.

What you have to do is to think of the one you wish to help, in order to set up a mental connection, and then go through the same treatment as for yourself, and at the same time forgetting your friend and losing yourself in getting a clear realization of. God. Suppose your friend is ill, you will establish a connection, and then turn to God, and what do you find? Instead of a clear realization and a flood of spiritual light, you find a great darkness which you cannot penetrate. (This is caused by your friend's illness, for illness is absence of God.) If, however, you will keep on denying the sickness and illness of your friend (but all the same not remembering your friend, for you must think only of God), and keep on affirming the Infinite Life and Health and Purity and Radiance of God you will gradually find the darkness will disappear until at last you get the clear realization and the flood of spiritual light. When that takes place your friend will be either cured, or, as is more often the case, partly cured, for it is usually a question of perseverance and persistence until the desired results are attained. This is the true art of Divine Healing, it is not done by suggestion or mortal mind, but is accomplished simply by the realization of the perfect purity and health of God.

In the same way you can "treat" each member of your family both night and morning, with the result that they will be kept from all evil and shielded from all harm, danger, disease and unhappiness. Also their characters will be transformed and changed into the Divine Image. Such "treatment" will ring harmony into the homes where humanly speaking such a thing is impossible. This "treatment" will perform the so-called impossible, or miracles, simply because it depends not upon any human or finite agency but solely upon God,

It will not keep people here beyond their allotted span, but it will make their lives happy and harmonious while they are here.

Proceeding in this way you will not only be able to make your own life happy, successful, harmonious and blessed, but you will. also be able to bring the highest good into the lives of others.

The vibrations of some persons are higher than others, therefore they make better healers, simply because they get a more intense realization, but everyone can help, not only himself or herself but also others. Some are so vibrant, even the gravest diseases give way before them, but while this is not possible in every case we can all be healers and blessers of others. And remember this, it is far easier to prevent disease than it is to cure it. It is not so spectacular, but it is much better to prevent evil than to cure it. When "treating" members of your family, you should deny all evil disease, sickness, ill-health, failure; and everything that you wish to protect them from, realizing that these things cannot exist in God. Then affirm their positive opposites and realize they are all in God and Divine Mind. Therefore "treat" daily, not only for yourself, but also each of your beloved ones in turn, separately. To do them in bulk is not so effective, although better than no "treatment" at all, each one should therefore be "treated" for separately. Healing by mental and spiritual treatment can only intensify, strengthen and help the healing forces of Nature. Nature is always trying to heal, and by "treatment," or constructive prayer, these efforts are helped and given a greater incentive. That is why materialists and doctors say at once, that it is a natural recovery. "Treatment" cannot make a new limb grow where one has been lost, it will not grow a new eye where one has been put out, or where the optic nerve has atrophied. It will not set a broken limb, but it will make it heal quickly and cleanly after it has been set by physical means. Mental Treatment and Divine Healing are wonderful, but they have their limitations, and if certain sects would remember this, they would be saved from much foolishness. Such being the case, it will be seen how much better it is to prevent disease than it is to cure it, also how necessary it is to "treat" spiritually, as early in the case as possible. The usual plan of trying every possible material "treatment" first, and then when given up to die, to call in a mental or spiritual healer, is not fair either to patient or practitioner.

In healing the sick it is not necessary to see them or to go near them, you may be hundreds of miles away and it will make no difference, for we are all in God (Divine Mind) and God is in us, and we all form one complete whole. Therefore it is as easy to "treat" a person hundreds, or even thousands of miles away as it is to "treat" one close to you. You will have an uphill task, however, if the one you are seeking to cure does not co-operate with you, by looking to God and trusting entirely to the influence of the Divine Spirit for healing. If you can get the patient to give up all belief in material means, and instead look only to God in the same way that you do, you will find your task very much easier. In fact, results will always be difficult to obtain unless you "teach" as well as "treat." Some will exclaim, "What about all the visualizing I have done, is that all in vain?" No, it is not in vain, it has served its purpose, and all that you have to do now is to visualize in God, instead of in man. By this you simply use your creative faculty in a higher plane. For instance, if you have been visualizing prosperity and plenty, you will now visualize and realize the Infinite Abundance of God. You will realize how wonderful and comprehensive is the plenty of the Divine Universal Mind. Perhaps you have been visualizing health, trying to see yourself a perfect and radiant creature, now, you will, instead visualize the infinite perfection and life and health of God and Heaven. So whatever it is that you need you will realize that it is in God, and as you realize that it is in God, so will the glorious knowledge and realization come to you that you are in God and that God is in you, that everything is yours, that there is only one complete whole, and you being in harmony with it, enter into possession of all good things. It is therefore only a question of time when these things must manifest in your life.

The reason why realizing that everything is in God supplies all your own needs, is because God and man are one. Everything that God is and has, man is and has, all that he has to do is to realize it. Therefore the real thing to aim at is realization, and this will come through the practice of the teaching of this Lesson.

Some students will ask, "But what about the special training of the subliminal mind?" This too has served its purpose, it has taught you to still the sense and listen to the voice within. That voice is the voice of God, and your Subliminal or Superconscious mind is the Infinite Mind of God incarnating in this flesh. Therefore you now realize there can be no separation from God. because God and man are one. Instead of saying, "My Subliminal Mind will solve all my problems," you will now affirm instead, "God is the solver of all man's problems." You get your own personality, which has been standing in your way and keeping Light, Truth and Understanding from penetrating your consciousness, out of the way, and find to your joy that you are in God (Divine Mind) and God is in you, that you are one. And being one with God makes you one with all things, all the beauties of the new day, the sweet air, the rising sun, the blue sky, the song of the birds, the fragrant blossoms, the sparkling dew, the radiant life all these are yours, and you are theirs, we are all one: one with one another and with God in the life of God.

You may also ask, "What about prayer, where does that come in?" The answer to that question is as follows: Realizing God is the only true prayer. If you examine the writings of all the saints and mystics that have ever lived you will find they all declare that the only true prayer is the realization of the reality and presence of God. The process of thought which leads up to this is not prayer, it is only primary prayer, or the pathway that leads to the real prayer. When the soul realizes the pure white light and radiance of spiritual glory, it knows that it has found God, not in some distant place, but within itself, and when it has found God it has found itself. Denials and affirmations are the quickest road to prayer, to that Divine realization by the soul, of the soul, which makes all things possible. Supplicating and begging things of God never bring any results, it is the prayer which is the realization that all things are accomplished, even before the prayer is made, that receives the answer. It is not a question of getting something, because all things are possessed already, it is the realization of this fact which produces what we call answer to prayer. Jesus taught his disciples how to pray, not to use vain repetitions, but to use a few denials and affirmations. Scholars tell us that the Authorized Version of the Bible does not correctly translate what is called "The Lord's Prayer," because it is impossible to give the exact Greek meaning in the English language. The old version, on the other hand, was made from a Latin translation and could not have given the correct meaning, because the Latin has no Aorist. Ferrar Fenton's translation is as follows: "Our Father in the Heavens; Your Name must be hallowed; Your Kingdom must be restored. Your Will must be done in

Heaven and upon the Earth." The form I like best is the following: "Our Father Thou Art in Heaven. Thy Name is adored. Thy Kingdom comes. Thy Will is done on Earth as in Heaven Thou givest us day by day our daily bread. Thou forgivest our offences exactly as we forgive the offences of others. Thou dost not tempt us but keepest us away from evil."

This was the prayer, consisting of denials and affirmations, which Jesus gave as a pattern. It is upon this pattern that my teaching is based. It is also upon this that all modern spiritual healing is founded.

In closing I have three things to say, and they are these: (1) Remember that if you keep on patiently working in the Unseen day by day, you are bound to get results in time. Do not refrain from working because you think you have not time, because you can find time if you make up your mind to do so. Let me use a homely illustration.

Supposing you had a small piece of ground and no time to dig it. If you said, I cannot dig this ground, I have no time," then the ground would never be dug and you would never get a crop. If, however, you said, "The ground must be dug somehow. I must And time," then you will find that in some way you will find time, even if it means getting up five minutes earlier, lacing up your boots more quickly and putting in only ten minutes at digging every morning. If also at night you took a lantern and did ten minutes more digging before going to bed, you will see that it would be a matter of time only before your plot of ground got completely dug. In the same way, if you can only snatch ten minutes night and morning, and work in the Unseen in the manner shown, there is bound to arrive a time when the result of your work will begin to show in your life and bring forth fruit after its kind. (2) When you have "demonstrated" the truth of this teaching and brought harmony into your life and family circle, do not get weary in well-doing and rest on your oars, and neglect your daily work in the Unseen, because if you do you will assuredly slip back, and your last state will be much worse than the first. Therefore, as long as your life shall last, do not omit ever to get in touch daily with the Unseen, and renew your spiritual life which is the source of all your power, success and health. Everything depends upon what you do in the Unseen, if you neglect this your life will begin to go wrong immediately. "First in the Unseen then in the Seen, this is the Law." Keep on for the rest of your life to work daily in the Unseen, and you will assuredly live a life of perfect peace, power and accomplishment. You will find that the realization of the Infinite Perfection of Divine Being will in time destroy all undesirable habits, great or small, should you have any, and by harmonizing with the Divine Will, all the weaknesses of the human will must pass away. In Lesson XII of Course I, it suggests that you go through the Course again. If you do so, notify it by the teaching of this lesson, thus cutting out the human "I will" and "I can" which were very necessary at the beginning, and replace them by the all-embracing "Thou Art." Also cease not to guard your thoughts and turn them into positive. Meet all difficulties by affirmations of Divine Power. Realize the Infinite Power of God and go forward and conquer. You can never fail, you are supported by the greatest of all spiritual powers. (3) Finally, many students have expressed great regret at the Course of Lessons having come to an end, and have said, "Cannot I keep in touch with you in some way? I feel lost and lonely now that the lessons have ceased coming." My answer is this, if each student will follow the teaching of this lesson, he or she can never be out of touch, for we shall all be vibrating, night and morning, at the same pitch. Every time that we work in the Unseen we shall be vibrating in sympathy with each other, and thus shall we be mutually helpful to one another. We shall all work more harmoniously in this way than if we met in the flesh, for the flesh is imperfect and deceptive, and gives a wrong impression, but mind, thought and spirit are eternal and permanent, real and perfect. Therefore, by working daily, night and morning, in the Unseen, according to the teaching of this lesson, we shall be in perfect harmony, and who can say what the result may be. For, vibrating thus in unison, we are not only benefiting ourselves, we are also making the world a better world, and humanity a better humanity through the power of scientific, directed, controlled thinking.

HENRY THOMAS HAMBLIN.

Within You is the Power

PREFACE.

There is a power lying hidden in man, by the use of which he can rise to higher and better things.

There is in man a greater Self, that transcends the finite self of the sense-man, even as the mountain towers above the plain.

The object of this little book is to help men and women to bring their inward powers of mind and spirit into expression, wisely and in harmony with universal law; to build up character, and to find within themselves that wondrous Self, which is their real self, and which, when found, reveals to them that they are literally and truly sons of God and daughters of the Most High.

There is no way whereby the discipline of life can be avoided. There is no means by which fate can be "tricked," nor cunning device by which the great cosmic plan can be evaded. Each life must meet its own troubles and difficulties: each soul must pass through its deep waters, every heart must encounter sorrow and grief. But none need be overwhelmed in the great conflicts of life, for one who has learned the great secret of his identity with the Universal life and Power, dwells in an impregnable city, built upon and into the Rock of Truth, against which the storms of life beat in vain.

While this little work does not offer any vain promises of an easy life-for, if this were possible, it would be the greatest of all disasters-but rather endeavours to show how to become so strong that life looks almost easy by comparison (the life or fate does not change or become easier, but the individual alters and becomes stronger), yet, it does show the reader how to avoid making his life more difficult than it need be. Most people's lives would be less filled with trouble and suffering if they took life in the right spirit and acted in harmony with Universal Law.

It is hoped that this little book may help many to come into harmony with life's law and purpose and thus avoid much needless suffering: to find the Greater Self within, which discovery brings with it a realization of absolute security: to bring into expression and wisely use their inner spiritual and mental forces and thus enter a life of overcoming and almost boundless power.

CHAPTER I. INFINITE LIFE AND POWER.

Man possesses, did he but know it, illimitable Power.[1] This Power is of the Spirit, therefore, it is unconquerable. It is not the power of the ordinary life, or finite will, or human mind. It transcends these, because, being spiritual, it is of a higher order than either physical or even mental. This Power lies dormant, and is hidden within man until he is sufficiently evolved and unfolded to be entrusted with its use.

Thought is a spiritual power of tremendous potency, but this is not the power of which we speak. By thought, man can either raise himself up and connect himself with the "Power House" of the Universe, or cut himself off entirely from the Divine Inflow. His thought is his greatest weapon, because, by it he can either draw on the Infinite or sever himself (in consciousness, but not in reality) from his Divine Source.

Through the Divine Spark within him, which is really his real Self, man is connected with the Infinite. Divine Life and Power are his, if he *realizes* that they are his. So long as he is ignorant of his oneness with the Divine Source of all life, he is incapable of appropriating the power that is really his. If, however, he enters into this inner knowledge, he finds himself the possessor of infinite power and unlimited resources.

This Power, then, is God's, yet it is also man's, but it is not revealed to him until he is fit to be entrusted with it. It is only when man realizes his oneness with his Divine Source that he becomes filled with Its power. Many teachers and initiates lament the fact that certain secrets are being spread broadcast to-day; secrets that, in the past, were kept closely guarded. They fear that unillumined and un-evolved people may make destructive use of spiritual power. This, to the writer, appears to be improbable. It is true that strong personalities, who have a great belief in their own power to achieve and succeed, draw unconsciously on hidden powers, and thus are able to raise themselves high above their fellows. The use, however, that they can make of spiritual power for base purposes is limited, and is not to be feared. There are others, of course, who are misusing their powers. These are black magicians, and while they may do a certain amount of harm, they become reduced, ultimately, to beggary and impotence. There are also others who spend the whole of their spare time searching for knowledge of this very subject. They read every occult book they can lay hands on, but they never find that for which they seek. There are spiritual powers and influences that withhold the eyes of the seekers from seeing, until they are ready for the revelation. When man, in his search for Truth, has given up all selfish striving after unworthy things, and has ceased to use his self-will in conflict with the greater Will of the Whole, he is ready for the revelation of his oneness with the Infinite. Yielding implicitly to the Will of the Whole may seem, to the unillumined, an act of weakness, yet it is the entrance to a life of almost boundless power.

Man is not separate from his Divine Source and never has been. He is, in reality, one with the Infinite. The separation which he feels and experiences is mental, and is due to his blindness and unbelief. Man can never be separated from Spirit, for he himself is Spirit. He is an integral part of one complete whole. He lives and moves and has his being in God (Universal, Omnipresent Spirit), and God (Spirit) dwells in him. The majority of people are unaware of this intimate relationship with the Divine, and, because they are unaware, or because they refuse to believe it, they are, in one sense, separated from the inner life of God. Yet this separation is only in their thoughts and beliefs, and not in reality. Man is not separated and never can be, yet so long as he believes that he is separate and alone, he will be as weak and helpless as though he actually were. As soon as man realizes the truth of his relationship to the Infinite, he passes from weakness to power, from death unto life. One moment he is in the desert, afar off, weak, separate, and alone; the next, he realizes that he is nothing less than a son of God, with all a son's privileges and powers. He realizes, in a flash, that he is one with his Divine Source, and that he can never be separated. He awakens also to the fact that all the Power of the Infinite is his to draw upon; that he can never really fail, that he is marching on to victory.

It will thus be seen how great is the power of man's thought. While thought is not the power of the Spirit, it is the power by which man either connects himself up with the Infinite Power, opening himself to the Divine Inflow, or cuts himself off and separates himself from his Spiritual Source. Thus, in a sense, man is what he thinks he is. If he thinks he is separate from God and cut off from His Power, then it is as though this were really the case, and he is just as impotent and miserable as though he actually existed apart from God. On the other hand, if he thinks and believes that he is one with the Infinite, he finds that it is gloriously true, and that he is really a son of God. If he believes and thinks that he is a mere material being, then he lives the limited life of a material being, and is never able to rise above it. But if, on the contrary, he thinks and believes that he is a spiritual being, then he finds that he possesses all the powers of a spiritual being.

Again, if he thinks that his work is difficult and that he is not equal to his tasks, he finds that really his tasks are difficult and beyond his powers. Yet on the other hand, if he believes his work is easy, or, at any rate, within his powers, he finds that such is the case, and that he can do his work with ease.

The power within is infinite, for, by faith in it, man is directly "coupled up" with the Spiritual Power of the Universe. The Divine Spark within him connects him to the Sacred Flame, thus making him potentially a god in the making.

A change then, must take place within man before he can enter into his Divine inheritance. He must learn to think after the Spirit, i.e., as a spiritual being, instead of after the flesh, i.e., as a material creature. Like the prodigal son he must "come to himself," and leave the husks and the swine in the far country, returning to his Father's house, where there is bread (of life) enough and to spare.

CHAPTER II. THE OVERCOMING OF LIFE'S DIFFICULTIES.

The true object of life is that man may attain wisdom through experience. This cannot be accomplished by giving in to the difficulties of life, but only by overcoming them. The promises of God are not made to those who fail in life's battle, but to those who *overcome*. Neither are there any promises that man shall have an easy time and be happy ever afterwards. Yet, it is after this that the majority of people are for ever seeking-an easy life, a good time, freedom from suffering and care. But, in spite of all their seeking, they can never find that which they desire. There is always a fly in the ointment of their pleasure, something that robs them of true happiness; or, possibly, combinations of circumstances conspire to upset all their plans.

Life is a paradox; the true object of life is not the attainment of happiness, yet if we attain the true object of life we find happiness. Those who are ignorant of life's true purpose and who seek happiness high and low, year after year, fail to find it. Like a will-o'-the-wisp, it for ever eludes them. On the other hand, those who recognize the true object of life, and follow it, attain happiness without seeking for it.

In times past, people have made God a convenience. They have thought they could drift through life, learning none of its discipline and then, when in trouble, or things were not to their liking, they could pray to God and have the unpleasant circumstances taken away. The same idea is prevalent to-day. People have left the old orthodoxy and look to various "cults" and "isms" to get them out of their difficulties. They do not believe now that they can curry special favour with God by prayer, but they firmly believe that they can get what they want from the Invisible by demanding it. They think that by this means they can have their own way after all. By this they mean having a good time, with no unpleasant experiences, trials, difficulties, adversities. They are, however, merely chasing rainbows. The easy life they seek constantly eludes them, simply because there is no such thing. The only life that is easy is the life of the strong soul who has overcome. His life is not easy in reality, but appears relatively so because of his strength.

It is impossible to have an easy life, and, if it were possible, then life would be not worth living, for the sole object of life is the building of character and the attainment of wisdom through experience. Life to all of us must always be full of difficulty, and it is to help those, who, hitherto, have found life rather too much for them that this book is being written. What the majority are seeking for is an easy life (which they will never find, but precisely the reverse) and for them I have no message. But to those wise and awakened souls who are seeking for Truth, no matter from whence it may come, and who desire to overcome life and its difficulties, instead of weakly giving in to them, this book, it is hoped, will bring a message.

At this stage we cannot go into the subject of why we should meet with disasters and adversity in this life, nor why some people should have, apparently, a smoother life than others.[2] We must therefore be satisfied to know that we have to meet trouble and overcome difficulty, and that it is only by so doing that we can attain wisdom and build up character. The question, then, is not *whether* we shall meet the trouble and adversity or not, but rather, *how* we shall meet them. Shall we be victorious or shall we be submerged? Shall we overcome life's difficulties or shall we give in to them?

The majority of people are drifters on the sea of life. They are wafted here and blown there: they are also carried hither and thither by every current. It is only the few who realize that they have the Power of the Infinite within them by which they can rise superior to all their difficulties, overcome their own weaknesses, and, through victorious experience, attain wisdom.

At this point some practical reader may say that attaining wisdom is all very well, but what he wants is practical help. He is perhaps out of work, has sickness in his house and is in debt. Or, he may be well-to-do, and yet in the deepest distress and misery. To all such I would say that they possess the Power by which they can overcome all their difficulties, and, through overcoming, attain wisdom. A man's success depends, more than anything, upon his faith-his faith in the good purpose of life: his faith in the Power of the Infinite within him and his ability to overcome every obstacle in his path.

The extent of the Power that man can bring into his life is the measure of his faith in that Power. If his faith in It is small, then his life will be feeble and lacking in achievement. If his faith in the Power within him is large, then great will be the power manifesting in his life. The Power of the Infinite is illimitable and inexhaustible: all that is required is an unquenchable belief and trust in it. The weakest and most timid can make use of this Power. There is the same Power in the timid and weak as in the brave and strong. The weakness of the former is due to a lack of faith and belief in the Infinite Power within them.

Difficulties and troubles there will be in every life, and sometimes disaster and heartbreak, when the very earth slides from under the feet, yet, by calling upon the Power within, it is possible to rise from the ruins of cherished hopes stronger and "greater" through experience. Happiness and true success depend upon how the troubles and difficulties of life are met. Adversity comes to all, but if it is met in the right manner even failure can be made the stepping-stone to success. Trouble comes to all, but, while it makes some people stronger and better in every way, it submerges others so that they never rise again. The trouble is the same, it is how it is met that makes the difference. Those who meet difficulty and adversity in the feeble strength of their finite minds and false personality are speedily overwhelmed and broken by the storms of life. But those who rely upon, and have faith in the Power within them, can never be overwhelmed, neither can they ever be defeated. The Power, being infinite, is always sufficient, no matter how great the need may be.

One who realizes his own real spiritual identity, knows that he can never die, that he can never be defeated, that he can never really fail. He may lose his body through the change that is called death; but he, the true man, can never die. Neither can he fail, though he be defeated a thousand times-he *must* rise again.

Only have faith in the Spiritual Power within you and you can know all the joys of overcoming and achievement. All things will become yours. Seek first the Kingdom within you (your spiritual union with the Infinite, and harmony with the Divine Will and Purpose) and all these things shall be added unto you. You will have no need to fear the morrow, for you will know that all provision has already been made. There will be no need to hoard up wealth, for there will be the necessary daily supplies always available. There will be no need to live near a doctor, for God, the Infinite Life, shall be your health. There will be no need for regret or lamentation, for you shall know that all is well. There will be no fear of future happenings, for you shall realize that the Infinite One makes no mistakes.

CHAPTER III. FATE OR FREE-WILL?

Great has been the controversy in the past, over the vexed subject of fate versus free-will. On the one hand, fatalists claim that man is so closely bound to the wheel of fate it is impossible for him to live his life in any different way than that which is mapped out for him. He can bring a quantity of first-class evidence in support of his claim and believes in his theory with all his heart. On the other hand, the advocate of free-will believes just as whole-heartedly that man is not bound at all, being as free as air. He, too, can bring plenty of evidence in support of his theory, which confirms him in his belief. Each one of them thinks that the other is wrong, yet they cannot both be wrong! Let us therefore examine the subject for ourselves, for it is an important one, being intimately connected with the subject which this book discusses.

First of all, let it be said, they are both wrong, in part, and right, in part. Man is bound to the wheel, yet, at the same time, he has free-will. Let us, therefore, explain this seeming paradox.

It is an ancient truth of the inner teaching that man, when he is unevolved and before he is "unfolded," is bound to the wheel of fate very closely. The unevolved man follows his desires, thus creating for himself a future from which he cannot escape. When however, he becomes more evolved and emancipated, he begins to resist following his desires and strives, instead, to follow higher things. This creates for him a better future and thus he becomes free in comparison with his former slave state. Man is a slave to fate as long as he is a slave to the desires of the earth plane. He is, however, free to overcome lower things and thus rise to higher. When he does this he ceases to create a painful future for himself and thus becomes free.

There is, therefore, fate which is self created. It is necessary to acknowledge this before we can proceed further. One who has not had much experience of life or who has not been a close observer, may deny that there is such a thing, but one who has had great changes in his life, against which he has fought and struggled in vain, knows that there is a purpose working behind the events of life, against which even kings and mighty men are powerless. There come times in man's life when he moves heaven and earth, figuratively speaking: prays until he can pray no more: sacrifices, it may be, his money, his health, his prospects, and does everything that is in the power of a human being in a vain attempt to stave off a threatened disaster. But, in spite of all his efforts, in spite of his cries to a pitiless heaven, the relentless march of fate cannot be stayed. It moves forward like a huge juggernaut and crushes his hopes, his dearest idol, his very life itself or all that then makes his life worth living-and leaves him desolate.

"If then," you may ask, "fate is so pitiless and so powerful, what can be done with it and where does free-will enter into the matter?" In reply it must be admitted at once that it is no use fighting fate. The more man fights it, the more completely he gets broken. There are certain main events in each life which must come to pass. These events and changes are inevitable and it is hopeless to fight against them. While these things, which constitute what we call fate, are inevitable and therefore cannot be avoided, it rests with ourselves how we meet these adversities and disasters. If we meet them in the wrong way they break us. If, however, we meet them in the right way we become stronger through discipline and experience, thus becoming better fitted to bear life's responsibilities and to overcome its difficulties and temptations. One who meets the setbacks, griefs, bereavements and disasters of life in the right spirit becomes a strong and rich character. He becomes mellowed through experience, strong, stable, a helpful influence to all who meet him.

When things go smoothly and life is a merry round, no philosophy or religion seems necessary, and "as for an inward power, what of it, we can do very well without it." So say the thoughtless and inexperienced, but there come times in every life, when, not only is a philosophy, and that a very sound one, necessary, but also a power, of which the finite self knows nothing, is needed in order to raise the soul out of the dust and ashes of its despair. It is one thing to try and meet trouble and adversity in the right spirit and quite another thing to have the power to do so. One who thinks that he has no power within him but that all the power is in circumstances, can never rise victorious over his troubles and become a conqueror over life's difficulties; but one who realizes that he possesses a wonderful power that can raise him up, no matter how crushed he may be, can never be a failure in life. No matter what may happen to him he will play the man and act a noble part. He will rise from the ruins of his life and build it anew in greater beauty and splendour.

At this stage it is necessary to point out that there is a difference between "big fate" and the circumstances of life. "Big fate" as it sometimes is called antedates this present life and its cause does not come within the scope of this little book.[3] Sufficient if we say here that, through the ages, we reap as we sow, therefore our future depends upon how we meet life and its difficulties *now*. Big fate, then, cannot be successfully fought, simply because it is the working of Omnipotent Law, but our life generally and its circumstances depend upon how we meet "big fate," and how we recover from it. No matter how seemingly unkind "fate" may be, it is possible for us to make our life a beautiful thing. Inspired and energized by the Power within, we can rise from the ashes of our dead hopes to build anew our life in greater beauty and more in harmony with the Divine Ideal.

Those who have studied the Occult sciences may say "what about planetary influences?" They will point out that, according to the ancient science of astrology, a man's life is determined by the "star" under which he is born. This is true, if he gives in to the influences around his path. At different times in his life man meets with influences that are sometimes "favourable" and at other times, adverse. These influences are, however, only influences after all, and one who will stand firm during periods of adversity and refuse to give in, relying upon the great Power within to carry him through, will find that he can weather all storms of life and come out of his trials greatly strengthened. He cannot prevent these influences from coming around his path of life, but he can rise superior to them. He will meet with failures and set-backs but he will make of these, stepping-stones to success. He will experience griefs and bereavements, but out of these he will build a finer character and rise to higher things. One, however, who gives in to these things, refusing to rise again and reconstruct his life, condemns himself to further suffering, thus making utter shipwreck of his life.

Let the despairing take heart again. Believe in the Power within you and you will rise to heights before undreamed of. With this Power to help you, you can accomplish the apparently impossible.

APPENDIX TO CHAPTER III.

Our life here is not governed by a capricious Being who blows first hot and then cold or who favours one person and tortures another. The Supreme Being works through laws that are absolutely just and unchanging. Therefore all disaster and trouble in the life is the effect of certain causes. These causes are our own wrong doing in the past, which set in motion forces, against which the power and wit and wisdom of man are powerless.[4] However, because the fundamental law of the Universe is love, it follows that the working of the law of cause and effect is not vindictive. Its object is our highest good, viz., to bring us into union with the Divine or in tune with the Infinite. Therefore, by rising up to a higher plane and coming more into harmony and union with the Divine, we rob even big fate of something of its power. We cannot oppose it, for by so doing we fight against Omnipotence, but we can *forestall* it by doing willingly, and of our own accord, that very thing which experience comes to teach us.

It will be seen then, that our future depends entirely upon the way we think and act in this life. Our future lies in our own hands. If we violate the law of love in this life, we create disaster and suffering for the future, which will have to be met, in the form of "big fate" of a painful character, some day. Therefore, by right thinking and right doing now, we not only ameliorate conditions in this life, but we also create a future that will be more harmonious and freer than anything we have experienced hitherto.

It is also necessary to point out that, even in this life, some of its big disasters are the result of thoughts and actions committed during this present existence. A youth or young man may commit a folly that brings, in after life, a terrible retribution. Or he may do another man a grievous wrong and years afterwards someone else does the same wrong to him. It is always an eye for an eye and a tooth for a tooth on this plane of cause and effect, but the Great Way Shower, by His teaching of the power of love, enables us to rise above these lower things and live a life of harmony and peace.

CHAPTER IV. CAUSE AND EFFECT.

Man is the cause of the disasters in his life. He reaps through the ages exactly as he sows. Life is perfectly just and rewards every man according to his works. The fate of the present is the reaping of his sowing in, it may be, a distant past. Therefore, the disasters and sufferings of this life, must not be attributed to the interference of a capricious and unreasonable God, for the truth is, they are due to the exact working of a perfectly just law. Fate, once created, is irrevocable. It can neither be fought nor evaded. By fighting against fate, man merely smashes himself to pieces. To do so, is equivalent to running his head against a stone cliff: the harder he charges, the greater the damage to his head-but the cliff is unaffected. Fate, although largely self-created, is really the Divine purpose of life: therefore, to resist it is to fight against God. Fate, again is not punishment, in any vindictive sense, it is the drawing together of certain remedial experiences, through which the soul can learn the lessons it has failed to learn in past ages and thus attain wisdom. The object of fate is the highest good of the individual, although it may entail suffering and painful experiences.

Because the disasters in man's life are due to past wrong doing, it naturally follows that his future depends upon the kind of life that he lives to-day. If, in the past, he has created for himself a sequence of events and experiences, from which it is impossible for him to escape, it is obvious that his future lives depend entirely upon how he lives the present one. It will be seen that if man can learn the lessons of the present life, and live in such a way as to cease creating trouble for the future, he is beginning to climb the Path of Liberation, which is the road all advanced souls have to follow, or, rather, have the privilege of following. By following this path, man ceases to be bound to the wheel of fate.

This little work does not teach reincarnation, but its teaching is based on a belief that man, in reality, is a spiritual being, a Divine Spark from the Sacred Fire. Spirit being immortal has no beginning or end therefore always lives. This present life is one of countless experiences, each one of which helps to build up character. There is no death, but only changes from one vehicle to another. There is no beginning, or end, or time in reality, these are mere limitations of the human mind. It is impossible for man to die: he can only leave his body. He cannot kill himself, try how he will: he can only force himself out of his body. Man must always go on, whether he likes it or not: he proceeds through the ages, *reaping exactly as he sows.*

We have already seen that man cannot avoid or fight successfully against fate, but that he can become free from the wheel of fate by living a life in harmony with Divine Law.[5] At this point it is necessary to point out that most of man's troubles are not caused by fate at all, but are due to his fighting against or trying to resist the great plan. If the experiences of life are resisted, or an attempt is made to evade its discipline, troubles and difficulties will repeat, becoming more painful and insistent until their lesson is learnt and the life changed accordingly. Therefore man has it in his power greatly to improve his present life, as well as to create a far better future, simply by living his life to-day in harmony with Divine Law. Further, it is necessary to point out that all thought and action have an *immediate* as well as a far reaching effect. It is true that the full effect of life here is not reaped until after our little course on this plane has been run, but great differences are effected in the present life nevertheless. The way a youth makes use of, or throws away his opportunities, either makes or mars, to a very large extent, his adult career. Opportunities, once allowed to pass, can never be recalled. Sins committed and wrongs done to our fellow men have an unpleasant habit of repeating themselves in a reversed way later in life. For instance, a man may get on in life, and, in his selfish climb, may trample on one weaker than himself, ruining him and driving him to despair. Years afterwards, he will probably be treated in exactly the same way by someone stronger and more favourably situated than himself. Therefore, there is an immediate sowing and reaping that finds fruition in this life. By "immediate" is meant, within the compass of this life. The reaping may be delayed ten or twenty years, but in the writer's experience, it not infrequently comes. "Whatsoever a man soweth, that shall he also reap." Those, therefore, who think that life is not just, and who whine and complain about the way they are treated, are simply increasing their own troubles. Until man realizes that the cause of all his troubles is within himself he can never do anything to remedy matters, because, obviously, the only thing that is required is for him to change within. Man has to become changed within before his life can be altered. His thoughts, his ideals, his attitude towards life must all become transformed. When this change has been effected, he not only begins to repair his present life, but he creates a fairer and nobler life for the future.

Man, then, has to change. His desires and aspirations, instead of being directed towards hate and evil must be transformed to love and good. Instead of wallowing in lust and selfishness he must lift himself to higher and better things. How can this be done? It cannot be accomplished by the finite man at all, but it can be achieved by the Infinite Power within. It is only when man realizes his oneness with the Infinite and *believes* that Omnipotent Power is at his disposal, that the Spiritual Power within becomes available. So long as man has doubts and fears or disbeliefs, this special power is not available. It is his, but his state of heart and mind prevents him from either realizing the presence of the Power or making use of it. Before the machinery of a workshop can run it must be connected up with the engine room. In the same way, man, before he can live the new life, must become one with the Infinite Life and Power.

Entering this new life of power, does not take away life's experiences, its trials, troubles and adversities, but the change within does prevent the creation of unnecessary troubles and suffering. Also even a so-called unkind fate loses much of its power to wound, for the higher man rises into union with God and Infinite Love, the less power it has in his life. It still operates, but it fails to wound so deeply, for man, seeing with illumined eyes, knows that it is good that has come to bless; and not evil that has come to slay. Painful fate loses its power to hurt when man ceases to resist it and meets it with open arms, seeking to learn the lessons that it has to teach.

CHAPTER V. SUCCESS.

What is meant here by success is the achievement of something worth while, that shall make the world better and richer, and add something to the common good. Our sphere in life may be very humble, but if we overcome our own weaknesses, help others along life's pathway, and do our daily work better than we need, our life cannot be other than successful. If, at the end of our life, we can be thankful for it, realizing that we have made the best possible use of it, we have achieved real success.

Success, to the unillumined, may mean the accumulation of wealth and the winning of fame. Yet those who give up their lives to the acquirement of these things are the greatest failures in life. They gain wealth, it is true, but they find that their money can buy only those things that bring no satisfaction: that it cannot purchase for them any of the things which are really worth having. Success of this hollow kind, can be won, but at too great a price. The greatest Teacher of all once said: "For what shall it profit man, if he shall gain the whole world and lose his own soul?" What *does* it profit a man if he "gets on" at the cost of happiness, health, joy of living, domestic life, and the ability to appreciate Nature's beauties and simple pleasures?

Yet man must be a striver. He must be for ever seeking better things and to express himself more perfectly. One who drifts through life, making no effort to rise to better things, is not worthy of the name of citizen. Man, if he is to be worthy of the name, must be for ever striving, overcoming, rising. Failure in life is always due to weakness of character. It is only strong characters who can resist the buffetings of life and overcome its difficulties. The man who would make his life worthy of respect and who would rise to high achievement and service, will be confronted by difficulty at every turn. This is as it should be, for it weeds out the weaklings and unworthy aspirants, and awards the spoils to those who exhibit faith, courage, steadfastness, patience, perseverance, persistence, cheerfulness, and strength of character, generally. Success, especially material success, is not, in itself, of much benefit to the one who wins it. It does not satisfy for long, but it is valuable in other ways. For instance, success, based on service, is a benefit to the community. If, it were not for successful people of this type the ordinary man in the rut would have a bad time. Also, the winning of success builds up character. One who would be successful in the battle of life, must be prepared to be tested and tried in every possible way. One who survives them all is built up in character in almost every direction. Even in his success, however, he will be tempted and tried. One who is engaged in the harsh struggle of business, or who takes part in public life, may, if he does not watch himself very carefully, become hard and callous. Of all failures this is probably the worst. One who succeeds in other directions and becomes a "hard man," is, after all, a sorry failure.

Again, people of the successful, striving, climbing type, are tempted far more than those who are afraid to venture and who remain in the valley of mediocrity. This is true, not only of those who seek to climb the steep path of spiritual attainment, but also of those who are successful in mundane affairs. In each case, they have placed in their keeping great powers and influence such as the ordinary man little dreams of. This is a grave responsibility, for if these powers are used for self-aggrandisement the results are disastrous. Thus, those who climb, are beset on all sides by temptations of a very subtle kind, which, if yielded to, will ruin the life and do grave injury to the soul.

Life is a continual battle. To the ordinary person it is generally a fight with circumstances and the ordinary difficulties of life which are very important in his eyes. The more advanced soul is not troubled much by these things-he rises above them-but he is tempted and tried to a much greater degree, and in a far more subtle manner. Those who think that by following a certain "cult" or "ism," they will be able to have an uneventful walk through life are merely deluding themselves. As he learns to overcome the difficulties of life which baffle the ordinary individual, he will be tempted and tried in other and more subtle ways. This is because life is not for mere passing pleasure, but is for the building up of character, through experience. Therefore, one who would succeed must be strong, and wise and patient. Those who aspire to make their lives really worth while: who desire to serve their fellows more perfectly: who want to build up character through experience and overcome all their weaknesses, inherited or otherwise, must look within for power and wisdom.

It must be pointed out, however, that man must not use his spiritual powers for selfish purposes and self-aggrandisement. There is an immutable law, which has been known to the inner teaching all through the ages, that forbids the use of spiritual powers for the creation of wealth or even of daily bread. Jesus was subject to the same spiritual law, and was tempted exactly in the same way as we. The tempter said: "Command this stone that it be made bread." If Christ had turned the stone into bread, He would have failed in His great mission, but He knew the law. There are thousands of people to-day who are trying, not only to turn, by the mis-use of their spiritual powers, stones into bread, but also into motor cars, fat bank balances and lands and houses. Such are heading to disaster, for they are working *against* the combined Spiritual Power of the Universe. The Enemy of Souls offers those who have learned to tap the inexhaustible Power of the Universe, and who have discovered that they are sons of God, wealth, power, pomp, the applause of men-the glittering things that perish-if only they will mis-use their God-given power. Like Jesus, they must refuse. They must put service before self, and give instead of grasping.

Thousands are being taught to-day to force their human will upon life and to use occult powers for the acquisition of wealth and power. They are taught to enter the Silence and demand "what they want." "How to get what you want" is the slogan of these modern teachers. Not merit, not service, not giving, but demanding, compelling by human will-power and by the use of occult forces. This is another device of the Enemy of Souls, and it is taking tens of thousands of seekers for Truth out of the Path. This subject is dealt with more fully in a separate chapter.

If, however, man's ambition is to serve and to give, instead of to grasp and to grab: if, also, he seeks success through merit and not through the mis-use of his spiritual powers, he can go forward and the Power will go with him and will help him. When once the Power has been aroused, man must cease all purely selfish striving, although, of course, there will still be much selfishness in his motive. He must seek his success through service and through following noble aims: through merit and a fair exchange, instead of trying to wring success from life, no matter who may suffer thereby.

Further, when this Power has been brought into expression it must only be used in love, for if it used otherwise it will destroy the user. Again, the Power must not be used by the finite human will, but an endeavour must be made to find what the Will of the Whole is, and to work in harmony with it.

Behind each life is the Divine Will and Purpose. Each life is perfect as it is imaged in the Universal Mind. The highest success, indeed, the only true success, is to live the life according to the great Cosmic Purpose, or, in other words, as it is imaged in the One Mind.

Do not imagine, however, that it is the Will of the Universal Mind that man should be a failure or lacking in achievement. Far from it, for we have only to contemplate the Universe to see that the Infinite Mind is for ever achieving and that it never fails. Man, too, must succeed, but let him mix wisdom with his ambition, and work for the benefit of the Whole, rather than for any purely selfish purpose.

It is natural for man to "get on" in life, to a moderate extent.[6] In order to "get on" he must become more efficient, and thus serve life and his fellows better. Therefore, there is no harm in success of this kind. It is natural and laudable also for one in poor and unlovely surroundings to have an ambition to raise himself to better circumstances. It is only right that he should desire to make life brighter and better for his wife and family. So long as he indulges in ambition wisely, and if he seeks success through *better service* to his fellows, his is a laudable purpose. If, however, he does not curb and control his ambition but allows it to "run away" with him, he will lose all real joy in life, and, at the last, when it is too late, learn, to his sorrow, that his life, through too much "success," has been a failure.

The writer's experience has been that it is necessary that we should always be progressing, achieving, overcoming and endeavouring to succeed. One of the greatest laws of the Universe is progress, therefore it is fatal to stand still. We must go forward, we must achieve, we must accomplish things. If we do so, we may find that many things which cost us much effort, and hard work are not worth the having, yet all the time we are learning, through experience, and are being strengthened and prepared for greater things. Through repeated failure to find true satisfaction we arrive finally at true knowledge, wisdom and understanding. We are wise then, if, with the world at our feet, we can be satisfied with a very moderate material success, and turn our attention and aspirations to higher and better things.

In concluding this chapter let it be pointed out that success and achievement will not drop ready made from heaven into your lap. All who succeed are gluttons for work, toiling whilst others play and sleep. All teaching to the contrary is erroneous. To think that success is going to come to you when it is unmerited, simply because you make use of "affirmations" or employ mental "treatments," is folly of the first water. On the other hand, to use the inner forces in an occult way, so as to compel material things or "success," so-called, in any shape or form, to come to you, is black magic. One who stoops to such practices becomes a black magician, earning for himself a terrible retribution. There is only one way to succeed in the affairs of life, and that is by raising oneself to greater usefulness and service. By doing things better than they have been done before, by bearing greater responsibility, you serve humanity better, and therefore merit success. "It is more blessed to give than to receive," said the Master, and this is true even in the practical and material affairs of life. First, you must give better and more valuable service: in other words, deserve and merit before you expect to see it materialize. You must sow before you can reap: you must become too big for your present position before you are capable of occupying a larger one. You must grow and expand in every possible way, and as you grow so will your success increase. Outward success is only a reflection, so to speak, of what you really are, and a result of greater and more valuable service to humanity. It requires great effort and determination to get out of the rut, but so long as your ambition is not ignoble or selfish, there will be found within you power sufficient for all your needs.

To win success, either in the hurly-burly of life, or the more difficult path of spiritual progress, demands imagination, vision, courage, faith, determination, persistence, perseverance, hope, cheerfulness and other qualities. These are all to be found within. All these qualities lie more or less dormant within, and can be called into expression if we believe that Infinite Power is ours.

Again, however, must the warning be repeated that this Power must not be used for selfish self-aggrandisement, still less may it be used, or, rather, mis-used, either to influence or dominate others. If this Power is mis-used the results are terrible and disastrous. Therefore, use the Power only for the achievement of good and noble aims and in service which shall enrich the life of your fellows, adding to the common good. Having arrived at this stage you must go forward. There can be no holding back. Ever onward, the Divine Urge is sending you, to greater achievement and accomplishment. Just as surely as the planets must revolve round the sun and fulfil their destiny, so also must you go forward. See to it, then, that your aims and ambitions are based upon eternal wisdom, for upon this does your whole future depend.

CHAPTER VI. HEALTH.

It is impossible, in a little work of this description to explain why it is that one person inherits a weak and ailing body and another enjoys a strong and robust constitution. Sufficient for us here to notice that the days of rude, rugged health are passing, and that man is becoming more highly strung, nervous and psychic in his make-up. The old type of rude, unconscious health was due to the animal-like nature of man, which caused his body to be governed more completely by the instinctive mind. Less evolved humans are not affected, apparently, by the mental storms, psychic changes, and spiritual disharmonies that disturb the health of the more evolved types. We have an illustration of this in the case of some forms of insanity. The patient "goes out of his mind," with the result that his bodily health becomes wonderfully good. The instinctive mind takes control of things, and rude, robust animal health is the result. When the patient was sane and his mind filled with worry, ambitions, plans, cares, lusts, hates and griefs, he was probably very far from well. This would be due to the disturbing effects of his thoughts and uncontrolled emotions. When, therefore, his conscious mind gave way and he became happy in an imbecile way, he ceased to think of these disturbing things, with the result that the instinctive, animal mind was able to work undisturbed.

It is of no use sighing for "the good old times," when people were rugged and strong in the way that savages are rugged and strong, for evolution has decreed that man shall change into a higher and more nervous and sensitive type. In this sensitive type wrong thoughts and emotions quickly produce pain and suffering. The majority of people do not know what good health is. Not only do they suffer from minor ailments, such as headaches, indigestion, rheumatism, neuritis, but they also never feel hearty or completely well. They are strangers to the joy of living. Life does not thrill them: nothing quickens their blood: they have no moments of vivid ecstasy-in other words, they do not live, they merely exist at a poor dying rate.

Again, the majority of people are susceptible to infectious diseases and epidemics, yet, if they were really well, they would be immune. Instead, however, of seeking immunity through health, they are seeking it through the use of vaccines and serums, thus adding to the burdens which the body has to bear. All attempts in this direction are bound to end in failure, for, as fast as one disease is suppressed another one will appear.

Many people look upon disease and sickness as inevitable, yet the truth is that health is the normal state and ill-health an abnormality. In tracing back ill-health to its source, we find, first of all, that it is due to disobedience of natural law. Large numbers of people break nearly every known natural law of health, and are surprised that they become ill. Yet the wonder is that they are as well as they are. Yet, while obedience to nature's laws and the use of nature-cure methods will carry us a certain part of the way, we find that there must be causes even deeper than those which are physical. We are confronted by the fact that there are many people who obey every known physical law of health, who bathe, exercise, breathe, eat and drink scientifically, who adopt nature-cure methods instead of drugs and serums, who yet cannot find health. Therefore we must search deeper and go to the mind in order to discover the cause of ill-health.

When we look to the mind we find a prolific cause of sickness. Man thinks himself into ill-health and disease. It is well known that thinking about disease and sickness produces them in the body. People who are for ever thinking about disease, illness, operations and other morbid subjects, become a prey to these things. Those who believe that sickness is inevitable, manifest it in their life. Morbid thinking produces a morbid state of the body, causing it either to fall an easy prey to infection or to break down into chronic ill-health, or even disease. Allowing the thoughts to dwell upon morbid things is a sure way to sickness and invalidism.

Man is not only made ill by his own negative thoughts and emotions, he is also under the hypnotic spell of the race mind. "The God of this world hath blinded the minds of them which believe not." We are all under the spell, more or less, of a huge illusion. The evil, disease, sickness and other imperfections that we see and experience, have no reality, *in reality*, but have an *existence* in *unreality*. [7]Although they are not real in a real sense, yet they are terribly real to this present limited consciousness. By realizing the truth, and by thinking and living in its light and power, the hypnotic spell becomes broken, not completely, else we should not grow old, but to such an extent that a state of greatly improved health can be enjoyed.

We are also hypnotically affected by suggestion, which reaches us from a thousand different sources. The conversations of friends and acquaintances, affect us adversely. Their belief in disease and sickness as realities, and in its inevitableness, colours all their conversation, and, unless we guard against it, this unconsciously affects us. Newspapers, magazines, books, all steeped in the same error, also influence us unless we have become too positive to be affected. From innumerable sources it is subtly suggested to us that disease, sickness, infection are realities that cannot be evaded, and to which we are prone. The effect of all this, putting it in simple and elementary language, is to divert the life power into wrong channels, thus producing disease and ill-health in place of perfection. The normal state of health has to give place to an abnormal state of disease or sickness. The normal health-state is, however, restored when Truth is realized, and the life lived in Its light and power. Absolute Truth and Perfection stand behind all the illusion and imperfection of the sense life. It is by realizing the Truth and the perfection of the Reality, and by establishing the thought-life in Truth, so that our thoughts cease to be negative and based on error and illusion, that health is to be found.

It is often said that ill-health is the result of sin. It is, for thinking about disease, sickness and ill-health, believing them to be inevitable, is one of the greatest of sins. The way of life is to walk (think and act) after the Spirit (which is perfect, whole, immortal and incorruptible) and not after the flesh (corruption, disease, sickness, death). By thinking "after the flesh" we dishonour God who is absolute Wholeness and Perfection, and cut ourselves off from the Divine Life and Power.

But there are other ways by which wrong thinking destroys the health. Thinking thoughts of lust is a prolific cause of unhappiness, sickness and nervous disease. The divine forces of life are directed into a wrong channel, resulting either in indulgence and inevitable weakening of body, brain and will, or in repression and its consequent nervous diseases. If the thoughts are allowed to dwell upon impurity, evil results must follow in some form, either in action or ill-health, or both. Thought must be controlled and reversed continually. Not repressed, but reversed, be it noted, for there is a tremendous difference between the two. Repression creates nervous trouble, but by reversing or transmuting the thoughts the life becomes transformed, and the bodily health greatly improved.

Further, indulging in thoughts of hate, resentment, ill-will, fear, worry, care, grief, and anxiety, produces ill-health, and, by lowering the tone of the body, lays it open to infection and disease. We therefore see that the state of the mind and the character of the thoughts are important factors which cannot be ignored. It is useless to treat either ill-health or disease if they are merely the external *effects* of hidden causes of the mind. In order to effect a cure we have to get back to the cause of the trouble.

Thought control[8] is a great assistance. Substituting a right or positive thought for a wrong one, will, in course of time, work wonders in the life. In the sub-conscious we have an illimitable power of extraordinary intelligence. According to our thoughts this wonderful power either builds up health, harmony and beauty in our life and body, or just the reverse. The power is good, the intelligence is apparently infinite, but it goes where-ever our thoughts direct it. By our thinking, therefore, we either create or destroy, produce either good or evil. If, therefore, all our thoughts are good, positive and constructive, it follows that both our body and our life must become built up in harmony and perfection. The question is, can this be done? It can be done if we have the desire, and are willing to discipline ourselves and persevere in the face, often, of seeming failure. Some readers may say, at this point, that they have no desire to be so frightfully good, that they are not prepared to give up lust, impurity, hate, anger, malice and thoughts and emotions of this kind. Very well, if this is so, they must go on and learn, through suffering, the lesson which they refuse to learn willingly. Others may say: "Yes, I want to control my thoughts, but how can I cease to worry when I have so much about which to worry, and how can I cease to hate when I have been so deeply wronged?" This brings us to an even deeper cause of ill-health than that of mind, viz., the attitude of the heart. Our scriptures tell us that "as a man thinketh in his *heart* so is he." By "heart" is meant the soul or feeling, desiring part of man. It is here where the conflict between the self-will and the Divine Will, between the desires of the flesh and the longings of the Spirit take place. The real root cause of all unhappiness, disharmony and ill-health is spiritual, and not merely mental or physical. The latter are contributory causes, but the former is the fundamental cause. Spiritual disharmony is, in reality, the cause of all ill-health and disease. Until spiritual harmony is restored, man is a kingdom divided against itself, which, as our Lord said, cannot stand. Healing, then, must be of a spiritual character. Until this harmony exists there can be no overcoming of hate thoughts, fear thoughts or worry thoughts, and until these are overcome there can be no true healing. Our Lord's healing was a gracious healing of the Spirit. It restored inward harmony by forgiving sin, by changing the heart's desires, by bringing the will of the subject into harmony with the Divine Will of the Whole. Our Lord's healing was not accomplished by means of suggestion, neither was it achieved by human will power; it was done by a bringing into harmony of the heart and desires and will with the Divine Will. At the same time there must have been a revelation of the truth that the Will of God is love, wholeness, joy and perfection, and not disease, sickness and misery.

Mental healing does not become possible until we have made our peace with God. Until we have surrendered entirely to the love principle, we cannot overcome our hate thoughts and malice thoughts or resentment thoughts, by transmuting them into thoughts of love. Until we surrender to the Divine Will and leave all our problems to the Infinite Mind, we cannot cease to worry and fear. Mental discipline and thought-control are necessary after this inward change has taken place, for we all have to work out our own salvation, but the essential thing is the inward heart surrender in love and trust. So long as we hate our brother, or fear what the morrow may bring forth, or worry about the things of this life, we can never be well. When, however, we have become attuned to the Divine Harmony, and have learnt to control our thoughts and emotions and to transmute fleshly and material desires into loving service, a state of wholeness is the inevitable result. Old, deeply-seated disorders die away, and a steady improvement in the state of health takes its place.

In order to regain health it is necessary to raise oneself up continually to the Divine Ideal of health, harmony and perfection. But this is useless if there still remains a clashing of the personal will with the Divine Will, or if there is any hate, malice, envy, or fear in the heart. The will must be surrendered to the greater Will (this, in reality, is our highest good, for the fulfilment of the Divine Will is the happy destiny of man): the heart must forgive and be filled with love; fear must be cast out, and replaced by confidence and complete trust, before we can enter into that happy, care-free, restful state which is necessary for healing. Health is harmony—a delicate balance and adjustment between spirit, soul, mind and body. This harmony is dependent entirely upon the greater harmony between ourselves and God. So long as there is a conflict of will, so long as there is hate or resentment, so long as there is selfishness or while there is fear, this harmony cannot exist. Therefore, the bed-rock cause of health is spiritual harmony, all healing being a restoration of harmony between man and his Divine Source. When this harmony is restored, man is no longer a kingdom divided against itself, for he becomes established in *unity*: he works with the Universe and the Divine Laws of his being, instead of against them. The Divine Life and Power flow through him unimpeded, promoting perfect sub-conscious functioning. His thoughts become cleansed at their source ("Create in me a clean heart, O God, and renew a right spirit within me," "Cleanse Thou me from *secret* faults"). He becomes free from the hypnotic spell of the race mind: his eyes, through the influence of the Divine Spirit, become opened to the Truth; therefore he is no longer blinded by the Prince of this world. In the Divine Union he becomes free. (In Christ all are made alive).

The subject of grief and its effect upon health has purposely been left to the last. No amount of right thinking will prevent bereavements in this life. These form part of the necessary discipline of life, and it depends entirely upon how we meet our trials whether they shall be hurtful or the greatest possible blessing. By rebelling against life's discipline, griefs become hurtful, but the hurt is not in the bereavement itself, but in the attitude of the mind and heart. Until the soul is able to drink the cup of sorrow willingly, and say "Thy Will be done," bereavement is hurtful, destroying both health and happiness. The cause of the hurt is, however, in the hardness of heart, and not in the bereavement itself. There must, therefore, be submission and an acknowledgment that the discipline is necessary. This does not imply, however, a weak giving-in to grief and mourning. One who has been bereaved can never, it is true, be the same again, for he or she becomes more chastened, more loving, more sympathetic, richer and more mellow in character. The loved one can never be forgotten, but that is no reason why the heart should be bowed down by grief and the life made desolate by sorrow. In such cases true religion, not religiousness, is the only thing that can satisfy the soul, harmonize the mind, and heal the body. To be established in Truth, knowing that all is well: that God makes no mistakes and that there is, in reality, no death but only change, is the only way by which bereavement can be made to be a blessing in disguise. When this stage is reached, grief is overcome, death being swallowed up in victory. The only panacea for all life's troubles is conscious harmony with our Divine Source and the Divine Will and Purpose which desire only our highest good.

CHAPTER VII. THE SECRET OF ABUNDANT SUPPLY.

It is a metaphysical truth that the outward life is a reflection of the thought life. Our life is affected by our habit of thinking and attitude of mind, in two ways: first, all our actions are unconsciously influenced by our thoughts, thus helping to bring into manifestation, or attracting to us, an environment that corresponds to our thoughts.[9] Secondly, we discharge or emit an influence, silent and invisible, that no doubt affects other people. They are probably not aware of it, but they are either repelled or attracted by this silent influence. Thus, if our thoughts and mental attitude are of the wrong type, not only are our actions affected thereby, but also we exert a silent influence that assists in driving the right type of friends, opportunity, success and every possible good away from us. The reverse also is equally true. By right thoughts and a correct mental attitude we naturally attract to us all the good of which our present life is capable.

The Bible tells us that as a man thinketh in his heart so is he. It is equally true to say that as a man *is*, so does he *think*, and, that as he thinks, so do his outer life and circumstances become. Therefore, as a man *is*, so is his environment. This may sound rather metaphysical, but it is really quite simple, and proof meets us at every turn. Take a man from slumdom and put him in nice surroundings, and note what happens. Very soon he either drifts back to a slum or turns his new house into a slum dwelling. Take a man of a higher type, and put him in a slum, and soon he will either leave the slum or change his slum dwelling into a more decent habitation. Put a slut in a mansion, and she will turn it into a pig-sty, but put a woman of a higher type in a hovel and she will make it clean enough to entertain royalty. Therefore, before you can change a person's environment it is necessary to change inwardly the person himself. When a man becomes inwardly changed and filled with new ambitions, ideals and hopes, he, in course of time, rises above his sordid surroundings and *attracts to himself an environment that corresponds to his new state of mind*. It would be useless to tidy up the house of a slut for her, for she would soon make it like a pig-sty again, but if you could get a new ideal of neatness, cleanliness, order and spotlessness into her mind, she would not rest satisfied until her immediate environment corresponded, in some measure at least, to her mental ideal or image.

Very often, the failures of a man's life, and its disharmonies and poverty, either comparative or real, are outward symbols of his weakness of character. He may have ability in plenty, but he may lack application or steadfastness, and thus he fails in all his undertakings, and has to be kept by his wife and daughters. He will assure you that his circumstances are due to ill-fortune, but the actual cause of his failure is in his character, or, rather, lack of character.

If, therefore, a man's poverty and lack, or financial difficulties are due to weakness of character which manifest in his work and dealings with others, in the form of inefficiency, poor service and bad judgment, it follows that he, himself, must change before his circumstances can be permanently altered for the better. The difficulty in dealing with unsuccessful people is in getting them to realize that they, themselves, are the cause of all their troubles. [10]Until, however, they do realize this, their case is hopeless, and it is impossible to help them, but when they acknowledge that the fault is theirs, they can be shown that there is a remedy for their ills and a way out of their difficulties, by means of self-improvement. Let them then search for hidden weaknesses, and build up those weak places in their character, such as lack of grit, determination, steadfastness, persistence, patience, probity, decision, which are the cause of their troubles, and they will find that their circumstances will gradually change for the better. Everything comes from within-first within, then out, this is the law-therefore the change must always take place within.

Going more deeply into the subject and becoming more metaphysical, it is necessary to point out that the cause of all manifestation is Mind. We have already seen that a man's mind and character are reflected in his circumstances; now let us think, for a moment, about the Mind that is Infinite. The whole universe, which is, of course, infinite in extent, has its origin in the Divine Mind, and *is contained within this Infinite Mind*, just in the same way that you can hold a mental picture in your own mind. God's Universe, *as it is imaged in the Divine Mind*, is perfect.

We see it as imperfect, because we only receive a finite sense-perception of that which is perfect and infinite, from this forming, in our minds, an image that is necessarily imperfect and finite, which we project outwards, and, not knowing any better, think is real. But the universe, *as imaged in the Divine Mind*, and as it actually is in reality, is both infinite and perfect: it is also infinitely perfect. There is no poverty or lack in a universe that is infinitely perfect, whole and complete in the Divine Mind. Poverty and lack have their origin in the mind of man: they have no place in the Mind of God.

We cannot, in a little elementary work of this kind, go more deeply into this extremely fascinating subject. Sufficient if we say here that the only Reality is infinite perfection and wholeness, therefore there cannot be any lack at all (in reality). The obvious lack and poverty that we see around us are the product of the human mind. Those who live in a consciousness of poverty and lack, go through life closely fettered by limitation. They can never escape from poverty, it dogs their footsteps like their shadow. In fact, it is a shadow or reflection, in the outer life, of their state of mind and mental attitude.

On the other hand, those who live in a consciousness of sufficiency, are not troubled about supply. Their circumstances reflect their type of mind and mental attitude. It does not follow that they will be rich, for many of them prefer to live from hand to mouth, and quite large numbers of people have no desire whatever to possess wealth of any kind, but they have no worry about supply, for their needs are always met by sufficiency.

Many of our readers look upon the possession of wealth as an iniquity. Personally, I do not see how, at this stage, it can be altogether avoided. Capital is necessary for the conducting of business and for the carrying out of enterprises, but, as far as the hoarding of wealth is concerned, I certainly think that it is both unwise and unnecessary. There is nothing more deadening to the spiritual life than riches. There is always hope for the drunkard and the harlot, but it is most difficult although, of course, not impossible, for one who is burdened by wealth to enter the kingdom of heaven. Some are able to do so, but they are allowed to enter simply because they hold their wealth as of no importance, merely as something of which they are stewards for a season.

The hoarding of wealth is just as unnecessary as poverty. They are both based upon a fundamental error. This error is in thinking that all supply, being material, must necessarily have a material source: that it is limited in quantity, and therefore must be grabbed at and fought over. The truth is, of course, that the source of supply is Spiritual, and therefore without limit; consequently, one who realizes the truth has no thoughts of poverty or lack, and ceases to fear it. On the other hand, he has no incentive to hoard or to grab wealth, for of what use are riches to one whose supply is for ever assured?

All who enter into this truth regarding supply, either despise riches or hold them very lightly indeed. They cease to have any desire for wealth. Why should they have any such desire? People hanker after wealth because they fear poverty with a deadly fear, and long for wealth because they think that its possession would release them from their fears. When, however, they know the truth, they also KNOW that their wants will always be supplied, therefore they no longer desire wealth and its cares and responsibilities.

Wealth is just as abnormal as poverty. Our Lord showed this to be the case by choosing to be poor (but not in poverty) and by His teaching in the Sermon on the Mount. What Jesus promised was adequate supply, but not wealth or riches, to those who had sufficient faith in their "Heavenly Father." Many people live this planless life of utter dependence upon their Spiritual Source. They never become rich, but all their needs are supplied. Something always arrives in time to meet their requirements. Such a life requires a very live and active faith, but its results are as certain as the rising of the sun.

An understanding of the truth regarding supply is a necessary foundation for the faith without which the planless life is impossible. It is necessary to *know* the utter falseness and unreality of poverty and lack before we can trust in Divine Providence or the working of Spiritual (at the same time, mental) law. It is necessary to know that the universe is Spiritual: that God is Spirit, in whom we live and move and have our being, and that because we are a part, very small, but yet a part, of the Whole, all our wants, all through the ages, must be supplied. Supply, sufficient for all our needs, is the reality. Poverty and lack, the product of lack of faith, of fear, of ignorance, of weakness of character, have their origin in the human mind, and are the unreality-the negative which has no permanence or reality.

When we have learnt the truth, it is necessary to live in the Consciousness of it, and to think and act and praise God as though sufficiency were already ours. Not to spend money that we cannot afford to spend, nor to incur debt, but to live mentally in an atmosphere of abundant supply. We have to remember that the change in consciousness must take place first and become well-established, before its effects can be seen to manifest in the outer life.

The entering of this higher consciousness where we know and realize the truth, viz., that the Source of all our supply is Spirit, and that the Divine Source is limitless, is not easy, although it is less difficult to some than to others. It demands constant mental activity and watchfulness: it requires persistence and perseverance in right thinking, yet it is possible to those who are in earnest. By living in the consciousness of God's Supply and exercising a lively faith, the life becomes affected, principally due to both conscious and unconscious change of action.

Having dealt with the esoteric or inner side of the subject of supply, I will now treat it more from the outer or practical side, the latter being, of course, just as important as the former.

The teaching of this chapter does not discourage industry and thrift, far from it. After the Lord Christ had fed the five thousand, all the leavings were carefully collected so that nothing should be wasted. This is in accord with Universal law. There is a law of economy both in the natural and spiritual worlds. Nature appears, on the surface, to be very wasteful and prodigal, but, actually, she never wastes anything, if it can be avoided. Therefore, the action of the disciples was in accord with universal law. What a lesson for us! To be careful and saving is a mark of superiority both in mind and character. The wastefulness of the helpless poor is notorious. Those who are "well to do" are far more careful and conserving than the very poor. There are exceptions, it is true, but the rule is that a man who cannot save money has not it in him to command success in life. Inability to deny himself certain things shows a weakness of character and lack of purpose which make success impossible. Two men that I knew very well built fortunes upon P5, which they saved out of meagre earnings. It is always the start that is difficult: if you cannot overcome the preliminary difficulties you have not the steadfast purpose to hold your own in the battle of life. On the other hand, once the initial difficulties have been overcome, it is not difficult to get your barque into the currents of prosperity. When once you realize that there is unlimited abundance in which you can share: when once you learn to live in the consciousness of this abundance, at the same time living within your present income and doing your present work as well as it is possible for it to be done, you have set out on the path to affluence. One who realizes and really believes that there is abundance and plenty for *him*, puts into operation a powerful law which will surely bring opportunity to him, sooner or later. Many, however, ruin their hopes by not knowing that for a time they must live a kind of double life. They must be opulent in consciousness, but careful and thrifty in actual practice. The time will come when their means will largely increase, then, if they are wise, they will live on part of their income, instead of living up to it. This will give them a wide margin for charitable purposes, for the taking up of further opportunities and for extensions. Many business men have to let golden opportunities pass, simply because they have saved little or nothing, owing to lavish private expenditure, or they have to let other people in to share their schemes who, in addition to taking a large share of the profits may prove a serious handicap and hindrance in other ways.

While in its essence, the Source of Supply is spiritual, it comes to us through material channels, and, in order to have a share in it, it is necessary to earn it. We have to give something in exchange for what we draw from life in the way of supply. We must give in order to receive, and what we give must be something that the world wants or needs.

The secret of supply is, then, to realize that there is unlimited abundance and to live in the consciousness of it, as completely as though no material channels existed, and, at the same time, to work as zealously and be as careful as though there were no such thing as spiritual supply. At the same time we must give the world something that it wants, or otherwise serve in some useful capacity, exercising honesty, probity and justice in all our affairs. It is folly to expect abundance to drop ready-made in our lap; it must be earned by intelligent and faithful service.[11]

Being a retired business man who started life with nothing, not even good health, I have looked at this subject from a business man's point of view. The principle applies, however, to every walk in life, and each reader can adapt the teaching of this lesson to his or her particular needs.

CHAPTER VIII. THE POWERS AND LIMITATIONS OF THE SUB-CONSCIOUS MIND.

The sub-conscious mind is the mind of Nature. It possesses extraordinary powers and intelligence, but no inspiration. It is instinctive: it is animal: it is natural: but there is nothing god-like about it-it is of the earth and the physical plane. It can be described as the inner forces of Nature resident within our body. Having said this we have said nearly all there is to be said about the sub-conscious, yet this is the mind of which some people have made a veritable god.

The sub-conscious mind, if led aright, is a very good friend, reducing all repeated thoughts and actions into habit, which, in time, become settled and part of the very life itself. Thus, by conscious right thinking and conscious right action, a good habit is formed, which becomes, in course of time, practically automatic. This, of course, builds up the character, which, in turn, affects the life. It will be seen then, how important is the right use of this willing and faithful servant. It is no god, it has no inspiration, but it is a very useful servant, as we shall see.

Most of our actions or movements are done or made sub-consciously. The reason that "practice makes perfect" is that the sub-conscious mind learns to do the task, and, by so doing, takes it off our hands. How difficult it is to learn to drive a motor-car. How carefully, at first, we have to double de-clutch and obtain the right engine speed for a noiseless "change," yet, after a time, the whole action is performed sub-consciously. It is the same with pianoforte playing. Many players, some better than others, can play the most difficult classical music without *consciously* recalling it to mind. As soon as they *try to remember* the whole "piece" leaves them, but as long as they leave the whole matter to the sub-conscious (which never forgets) they can keep on playing. I and my conscious mind are not doing much of the actual writing of this book. We think the thoughts and have something to do with the formation of the sentences, but the sub-conscious mind writes them down. If I had to think of each word and letter, my task would be hopeless, and I should become half dead with fatigue.

The sub-conscious mind, however, is even more helpful, for it does the bulk of our thinking, and can be taught to do a great deal more. If we had to think everything out laboriously, according to the laws of logic, life would be unbearable. Instead of this our sub-conscious mind does the bulk or our thinking, and, if we give it a chance, will do it in an extremely accurate manner, strictly according to the laws of logic and *without the slightest fatigue.* The more that we train the sub-conscious to do our ordinary thinking for us, the less we suffer from fatigue. Fatigue is unknown to the sub-conscious mind, therefore we can never tire it or overwork it.

The sub-conscious mind can be made to do more and more work for us if we will delegate definite work for it to deal with. One who has learnt thought control, who can take up a matter, consider it in all its bearings, and then dismiss the subject from his conscious thought, is able to increase his efficiency a hundred per cent., and reduce his mental fatigue almost to vanishing point. Instead of laboriously working out his problems and worrying and scheming over them, he simply dismisses them to his sub-conscious mind to be dealt with by a master mind which works unceasingly, with great rapidity, extreme accuracy and entirely without effort. It is necessary, however, to give the sub-conscious every available information, for it possesses no inspiration or super-human wisdom, but works out logically, according to the facts supplied to it.

This great, natural, untiring "mind downstairs," as it has been called, is also capable of doing even more useful work still. A writer or speaker, or preacher can collect notes and ideas for his article, book, speech or sermon, and pass them down to his sub-conscious mind with orders that they be arranged in suitable order, division, sub-division and so on. When he comes either to write or prepare the notes of his speech or sermon, he will find all the work done for him, and all that he has to do is to write it down, entirely without effort or fatigue.

Again, a business man who has learnt to make use of his sub-conscious mind in this way, need not juggle or worry or fatigue himself by planning and scheming for the future. All that he need do is to submit the facts to the "greater mind downstairs," and all the planning will be done for him, entirely without effort, and far more efficiently than he would have done it through laborious conscious thinking.

The following, which has just been brought to my notice, is a striking confirmation of the teaching of this chapter.

In a recent issue of *Collier's Magazine*, an interview with Henry Ford appeared. He spoke of the way with which big business men deal with problems, and pointed out that they did not spend a lot of time pondering and puzzling over plans or ideas. He said: "An idea comes to us: we think of it for a little while, and then *we put it in the pot to boil*. We let it simmer for a time, and then take it out." What Henry Ford means, of course, is precisely what we have been saying, viz., that the idea or problem is dismissed to the sub-conscious mind, which works it out, and presents it to the conscious mind for judgment.

Yet again, an inventor or one who is constructing something mechanical, can make use of the sub-conscious mind in precisely the same way. Let him sum up the whole problem, arrange all his facts and available information, and pass them all to his sub-conscious mind, when, if a successful result is within the range of possibility, an answer or idea will be forthcoming. All this being done, mark you, without any effort whatever.

All this may seem, especially to some readers, rather wonderful and far-fetched, yet there is nothing occult or mysterious about it. I am perfectly sure that there is no great writer, politician or business man who does not make use of his sub-conscious mind in this way. He probably does so unconsciously, but his procedure is the same. Some employ the whole of their mind naturally. These become men of achievement, who occupy responsible positions, and who bear immense burdens without strain, worry or care. Responsibility sits lightly upon them, and they are serene and untroubled when in positions, and when confronted by tasks and difficulties, such as would drive an ordinary individual out of his mind. Such men develop their powers of attention and concentration (anyone who is in earnest can do this) to a very high degree. They are at great pains to get to the root of a problem, and obtain all the available data possible, but, after that, it is their sub-conscious mind that does all the work, and which arrives at a decision.

While it comes natural to a few to use their sub-conscious mind in the correct way, the majority of people find themselves unable to do so. Such, however, can acquire the art by training. First, it is necessary to learn thought-control, so as to be able to take up a problem or dismiss it entirely from the mind *at will*. When a problem is passed on to the sub-conscious to be worked out, the subject must be dismissed entirely from the conscious mind. The problem must not be worried over, nor the thoughts allowed to dwell upon it; it must be left entirely to the sub-conscious. Second, every possible detail and information connected with the problem must be grasped by the conscious mind, and the whole matter, pro and con, visualized before being passed to the sub-conscious. It will be seen, then, that thought-control of a high order is necessary, also powers of attention and concentration. These can all be developed by anyone who is really in earnest.

A good way of starting the use of the sub-conscious mind is to hold the problem in the mind just as one is going to sleep. There must not, upon any account, be any attempt made to solve the problem or to worry over it. Instead, the main facts of the case, on both sides, must be marshalled, and the case presented to the sub-conscious mind in much the same way as you would place it before your lawyer. Having done this, dismiss the whole matter to your sub-conscious mind, and in most cases you will find in the morning that a solution has been arrived at without any effort or fatigue on your part.

This, of course, is only one of the many ways in which the sub-conscious mind can, and does, serve its master, or the one who should be master. This great invisible force of Nature is for ever working. Whatever ideal is held in the mind becomes woven into the life through the tireless working of the sub-conscious mind. Only set your attention upon high and lofty achievement, and you will focus all the invisible inward forces of Nature upon its accomplishment. In course of time you will reap as you sow. If you will direct your attention into the right channel, backing it up with energetic, conscious action, your sub-conscious will help you day and night, thus making success and achievement possible.

CHAPTER IX. THE USE OF THE SPIRITUAL OR SUPER-CONSCIOUS MIND.

We have already seen that the sub-conscious mind, wonderful though it be, is instinctive merely, lacking inspiration and what we call originality.

All inspiration comes from the Universal Mind, via the super-conscious.

All poets and inspired writers get their inspiration in this way.

This higher mind is not recognized by Psychologists, but it has long been known to searchers for spiritual truth.

What we get from the sub-conscious is the outcome of facts and knowledge supplied to it. What we get from the super-conscious is direct inspiration from higher planes. This higher mind might also be called the Mind of Illumination, for those who can enter into it become illumined, being able to know the Truth and to see things as they really are, and not as they falsely appear to the senses.

This limited consciousness in which we live is bounded by our five senses. The universe that we see around us is partly real and partly an illusion. The real universe is Spiritual and infinite: what we sense is a limited, partial conception of a fragment of it. Our limited, finite conception of the universe is entirely misleading and erroneous, and so long as we rely on sense evidence and the human mind, we remain in darkness and uncertainty. When, however, we can rise into the super-conscious realm, our consciousness expands, transcending the senses and the limitations of the physical plane.

The Spiritual mind is, of course, only accessible to those who are more delicately attuned to its finer vibrations. Nothing that is worth having can be had without effort, and it is only after much self-discipline that it becomes possible for the student to raise his consciousness to this higher realm and understand life from the standpoint of the Universal Mind.

There is nothing, either mystical or psychical, about the use of this higher mind. One who makes use of it becomes spiritually-minded, that is all. He does not go into trances, nor need he become clairvoyant: he simply remains a sane, normal individual, with this difference only-he makes use of more of his mind than does the ordinary individual.

One who is able to use this higher mind develops that which has been termed "the divine quality of originality." If ever a person is to rise above the dead level of mediocrity it must be through direct inspiration from higher planes, through his super-conscious mind. If ever a person is to bring forth a new idea which shall enrich humanity and add to the common good, it must come through the higher mind.

One who is properly attuned, becomes, through the super-conscious mind, a recipient of knowledge that is above human, and wisdom that is divine. He knows by direct knowing: he becomes wise through an influx of Divine Wisdom. He is able to distinguish between the real and the sham, between the gold and the dross: he is also able to see and recognize the right path in life —a thing utterly impossible to the mind of the senses-and to tread it, thus being led into the only true success and real good of which his life is capable.

Let it be said here that all Wisdom must come from within. While books and the written word may be helpful, it is the Spirit within the reader that illumines the word, and makes it real and true to the seeker after Wisdom. One who realizes that he is illumined within by the Divine Spirit, and that this alone can bring him into real knowledge is well advanced on the path that leads to realization.

The wisdom of the human mind always leads to disappointment. It is based on the evidence of the senses, which is erroneous, therefore its findings must always be lacking in *real* wisdom. One who relies upon the inspiration of Divine Wisdom has often to decide to take a course of action which, apparently, is opposed to his best interests. Yet, if he follows the inward Wisdom, he finds that he is always guided aright, and, later, has cause to be devoutly thankful that he followed the gleam.

CHAPTER X. CHARACTER BUILDING AND THE OVERCOMING OF HABIT.

Character building is the greatest object in life. It has been said that character is the only thing we can take with us when we depart this life. This is perfectly true, therefore the object of all religion (not religiousness), mental training and development should be the building of character. A religion that does not build up character is worthless. Those who think that they can "flop" through life, avoid, as far as possible, its discipline, make no effort to improve their character, and through believing in a certain creed can miraculously become perfect, simply by dying, are deceiving themselves. We do not become "perfect," *i.e.*, of a strong and perfect character, either by believing in a creed or through dying, but by attainment. God helps those who help themselves, and those people who will not strive after better things cut themselves off from all the glorious and wonderful possibilities of attainment.

Before, however, thinking about such lofty things as entering the Path of Attainment, and becoming changed into, and modelled after the Divine Image, the average person may wish to know how to overcome bad habits and weaknesses of character which are keeping him down in life, and, possibly, undermining his health. Most people are conscious of some wrong habits that ought to be overcome, and weaknesses of character which should be eradicated. Possibly they have fought against their habits or weaknesses for years, prayed until they are tired of praying, made innumerable attempts at turning over a new leaf, yet all in vain, for they are as firmly in the toils as ever. Many people give up the struggle and endeavour to lead a sort of Jekyll and Hyde existence, being outwardly a Christian or righteous person, but inwardly something quite different. Yet they find no satisfaction in this dual life, for they know that they are drifting towards an abyss.

Yet there is a way of escape that is open to all. The Infinite One has provided man with powers that are apparently unlimited: powers which can be used either to build up the life and character or to destroy them. These powers are those of the sub-conscious mind. This mind is a reservoir of unlimited, tireless forces, and becomes, if we use it aright, our best friend, or, if we mis-use it, our worst enemy.

Every time a bad action is indulged in, wonderful changes take place in the nervous system, and energy becomes stored up in certain cells, so as to make it easier to do the wrong act on a future occasion. It is equally true that every time a good action is done, similar changes, but in a reverse direction, take place, that make the doing of the same action easier in the future. This explains the tremendous power of habit. Our body, brain and nervous system become changed, either for the worse or the better, according to the type of action indulged in.

We do not yet fully realize what a wonderful adventure life is. We are entrusted with tremendous powers, and by their use or mis-use we can either destroy ourselves or build up our character in every possible direction. What a responsibility, yet what a glorious opportunity!

In order, however, to find a way of escape from evil habit and weaknesses of character, we must go deeper than actual deeds, for actions are effects of hidden causes. The cause of all action is thought. A thought, someone has said, is an action in the process of being born. It is true that we possess primitive desires and impulses, but these can be transmuted into noble actions and high achievement simply by directing the thoughts and attention to higher and better things. For instance, the powers of sex become transmuted into brain power if the thoughts and attention are completely transferred from sex to intellectual pursuits. If, however, the thoughts are allowed to dwell upon sex or passion, then the kingdom becomes divided against itself, and man begins to drift towards the abyss. The strain of modern life is filling our asylums, yet there are those who can work fifteen or even eighteen hours a day and thrive on it, although engaged in severely-trying brain work. These have learnt to transmute their lower powers into higher. This is not done by means of esoteric or occult practices, but by obeying the Divine Injunction to set our affections on things above. In other words, to keep our thoughts and attention fixed upon higher and better aims, ambitions and pursuits.

It is impossible to overcome bad habits by fighting them, for the more we fight them the stronger they become. The injunction to "resist not evil" is very applicable to habit. The way of escape is not by fighting evil or wrong habit, no matter what its character may be, but by concentrating upon building a good habit that shall cut the ground from under the feet of the bad one, or by turning the attention to higher and better things.

Whatever we fix our attention upon, or whatever it is that we idealize, our sub-conscious mind endeavours to actualize and make real in our life. By fighting a habit we direct sub-conscious attention to it, and this is fatal. If, however, we turn our whole attention to something entirely different and which is higher and better, all the powers of the sub-conscious are directed towards the production, in the life and body, of the new object of attention.

We see, therefore, that we do not have to overcome habit. If we did our task would be hopeless, for the human will is helpless before the power of the sub-conscious mind. The sub-conscious powers can be led by the imagination, but they cannot be coerced by the will. The will must be used not to fight the habit, but in raising and directing the attention to something higher and better. By this means a new habit is formed. The attention of the sub-conscious mind is taken away from the bad habit, and all its powers directed towards the creation of a new and better one. The sub-conscious does not care what the habit is. It is indifferent as to whether it is good or bad. It is just as willing to produce a good habit as a bad one. We, each of us, therefore, hold our fate in our own hands. We can, by controlling our thoughts and imagination and by directing our attention to better things, focus all the powers of the sub-conscious on the building up of good habits, or, on the other hand, we can, by allowing our thoughts and mental pictures to dwell upon undesirable things and our attention to be directed to low or weak ideals, fall into undesirable habits. The power that produces the habits is the same in each case; it is the way in which this power is directed that is the vital and essential thing.

It is very necessary to point out that right thinking and correct use of the imagination must be accompanied by corresponding right action. Many people make use of auto-suggestion and expect it to destroy their bad habits and build up better ones, but it never will, or can do so, unaided. Auto-suggestion is useless if it is not followed by constructive action. Young people should expend their energies in physical culture and games. Older people should interest themselves in hobbies and intellectual pursuits. It is only advanced students who can control their thoughts so that they can govern their life forces by mental means. Those less advanced, when attacked by evil or weak thoughts, must get up and *do* something quite different, and thus get their minds off the forbidden subject and interested in the new object of attention. It is a case of directing the desires and life forces into different channels, by controlling the thoughts and attention. Here is seen the value of true religion, for it brings fresh ideals into the life and directs the attention to higher and better things. The writer realizes that a change must take place in the heart of the individual before he can desire these better things. When, however, this change has taken place, the battle has only just begun, for each one has to work out his own salvation.

At first, then, most people will find it necessary to do something in order to attract their attention and guide their thoughts to something quite different from the forbidden subject. Later on, however, when they become more advanced in the science of right thinking, they will be able to direct their thoughts into any desired direction. This necessitates constant vigilance. Each thought has to be carefully scrutinized before being allowed to pass the threshold of the mind. By reversing every negative or unworthy or ignoble thought into its opposite, a change is wrought in the brain and nervous system. The cells formerly used for wrong thinking and for the production of wrong action go out of use as new cells are brought into use for the production of right action.

This stage leads to one higher still, when it becomes a settled habit to reverse bad thoughts into good ones and perform right actions instead of bad or weak ones. The power of the sub-conscious mind, which at one time seemed so evil, produces right action more or less automatically. When once the habit of cleaning the teeth is established there is experienced an uncomfortable feeling until they have been attended to. When once a dirty person has learnt to wash himself thoroughly and keep himself decent, he will feel uncomfortable if he gets dirty. The same rule applies in the more important things and habits of life. If those who are in the bondage of habit will only direct their thoughts and attention to the building up of good habits, their old weaknesses will die a natural death.

It must not be thought that the victory over life-long habits is easy. It may seem so at first, but sooner or later temptation will come with added force, which may result in a sad fall. If this should happen it is most important that too much attention should not be paid to the incident. Instead, the beginner should pick himself up, and, making a mental note of the immediate cause of his downfall, thus benefiting by the experience, press on again towards freedom. It is most helpful to realize that not only is the sub-conscious mind willing to be guided aright, if we will only persevere long enough (until persevering itself becomes a habit), but that we also have behind us all the Spiritual powers of God. The Infinite One sees to it that the odds are not overwhelmingly against us. Our difficulties are not insuperable, although they may appear to be so. We can always win through if we faint not. Heaven looks on with sympathetic interest and rejoices with the struggler when he succeeds, and mourns with him when he fails. The struggle is a stiff one, for it is only by this that the seeker after God can become strong in character, but the victory can always be won. When the situation appears hopeless, let the struggling one remember that there is a way of escape somewhere, and that God, who is his freedom and deliverer, will reveal it to him if he faints not. If all who seek deliverance will realize that the Power of the Infinite is on their side, and that they are bound to become victors if they will only keep on, they must succeed. And what a joy is theirs! There is no happiness quite like that which comes to one who has fought the good fight and overcome habit and weaknesses of character.

May every reader experience this supreme joy of overcoming.

CHAPTER XI. HAPPINESS AND JOY.

Deep down in every heart is an unquenchable desire for happiness. The advanced soul desires happiness just as much as the pleasure-seeking worldling, the difference between them is simply that the former, through knowledge and experience, does not search for happiness, knowing that it can never be found by direct seeking, but finds it through service and love to others and in victory over self; while the latter seeks happiness, like a will-o'-the-wisp, in every form of pleasure, and finds it not.

Man is never satisfied with his life: he is for ever seeking something that is better. Until he learns wisdom, he looks for it in pleasure, in sense gratification of various kinds, in wealth, luxury and possession. The less evolved a man is the more convinced he is that happiness can be gained in these ways, and the lower are his desires. For instance, those who form what is called the underworld of our cities, seek happiness in vice and debauchery. Those who are more evolved seek pleasure in more refined things, hoping to find happiness in intellectual pursuits, friendships, and in pure human loves. These more evolved types get much more pleasure through the senses than do those who are more elemental, but they are capable also of greater and more acute suffering. They can derive great pleasure from a picture gallery, whereas a savage would see nothing interesting at all: they can also suffer from things which a savage would not be capable of feeling. Yet, in spite of this developed refinement and ability to derive pleasure from art, science, literature, etc., happiness is still as far off as ever. All attempts at finding happiness lead finally to "emptiness." There is no satisfaction, either in wealth and all that it can command, getting on in life, or in fame and power. They allure at first and promise happiness, but they fail us, and finally are seen to be but vanity and vexation of spirit.

This desire for happiness is good, for it leads us through innumerable experiences so that the soul can realize, by practical experience, the emptiness of all self-seeking, and thus learn wisdom. After running the whole gamut of experience the soul learns at last that happiness is not something that can be found by seeking it, but is an inward mental state.

Although work, well done, brings a quiet sense of satisfaction, and success in one's career may also be a source of gratification for a short time, yet even these cannot satisfy the deep longing of the soul.

Happiness, however, is to be found in service. Not if we seek happiness in service, and serve in order to be happy, but if we serve others for the sake of serving we find the only happiness that will endure and satisfy.

One has only to observe the lives of those who are always selfishly seeking and grabbing, who are hard in their dealings, and always "looking after number one," in order to see how impossible it is for self-seekers to be happy. It does not matter whether they acquire riches or remain poor-they are equally unhappy. In contrast to this, you have only to go out of your way to do a kind and perfectly disinterested action and experience the glow of sheer happiness that it brings, in order to realize that you are dealing with a law of life that is as sure and unalterable as the law of gravitation.

There must be a purpose in life, and this must have for its object the betterment of the lives of others, either few or many. The law of service must be obeyed, otherwise there can be no happiness. This may fill some readers with dismay, for they may be employed in an occupation that apparently does no good to anybody. They may feel that if they were engaged in some noble enterprise for the uplift of humanity, then they could truly serve, but in their present occupation this is impossible. To think thus is very natural, yet the truth is we can all obey the law of service, and can begin now, in our present occupation, no matter what it may be. We have only to do our daily work, not as a task which must be "got through," in order to bring us a living, or because it is expected of us that we should work, but as an offering of love to life and the world, in order to come into harmony with the great law of service. Our ideas of values with regard to occupations are altogether erroneous, from the "inner wisdom" point of view. The scrubbing of a doorstep, if faithfully done in a true spirit of service, is of as much value and real importance as the writing of a deathless poem, or dying for one's country. We can never truthfully say that one act of service is of greater value, or is more important than another. All that the higher law looks at is the *motive*. Therefore, if your motive is right, you can be engaged in the humblest and, apparently, most useless occupation, and yet be happy because you satisfy the law of service.

Another road to happiness is the conquest of the lower nature, the overcoming of weaknesses, the climbing to higher and better things. There is intense happiness in realizing daily that old habits are being overthrown, weak points in the character built up, and an ever-increasing state of liberty and freedom entered into. Thank God, we do not have to remain as we once were, but can progress upwards, indefinitely, for there is no limit to our upward climb.

But there is a state that is far higher than happiness, and this is JOY. Happiness comes through service and overcoming, but joy comes only to one who realizes his oneness with his Divine Source. The *reality* is ineffable joy. Behind this world of shadows is the real, spiritual world of splendour and delight. When the soul, after its immense journey through matter, time and space, at last finds its way back to its Divine Source, it becomes aware of this intense joy, too great to be described in words. It not only realizes that the *reality* is joy, and the universe filled, not with groans or sighing, but with the sweet, quiet laughter of freed souls! it also is filled itself with this ineffable joy.

What has all this got to do with practical, everyday life, it may be asked? Everything, for the one who possesses this quiet joy can never be defeated in life's battles. He has something within him that can never be quenched and which will lead him from victory to victory.

CHAPTER XII. THE USE AND MIS-USE OF MENTAL AND SPIRITUAL POWERS.

The average individual knows nothing of mental forces, and, although he may suffer from the effects of unconscious wrong thinking, yet he is in no danger of making deliberate mis-use of the inner powers. One, however, who has learnt how to use these interior forces must be very careful to use them aright or he will find that the invisible powers of mind and spirit are far more powerful and destructive than dynamite. It is not meant by this that he can blow himself up thereby, but it does mean that he can injure himself, not only in this life, but for ages to come, and, in addition, seriously retard his spiritual evolution.

All use of the mind to coerce other people or to influence them by means of suggestion, not for their benefit, but for your advantage, is highly destructive, not to them actually, *but to you*. On the face of it, it looks an easy road to success and prosperity, but, actually, it leads to failure and poverty. The mis-use of the mental powers in this way is really a form of black magic, and the fate of all black magicians is very terrible. Even the use of the mind to coerce other people *for their good* is not desirable. It never does any real good, although it may seem beneficial for a time, and its use, therefore, is to be deprecated. Healing, so-called, by hetero-suggestion, is not permanent, for as soon as the healer ceases to "pump" suggestion into the patient the latter begins to relapse into his former state. Far better results accrue if the patient is taught to use auto or self-suggestion for himself. It is seen, then, that the use of the mind to influence others is distinctly harmful if it is used selfishly, and of no real use if used unselfishly. Hypnotism is harmful, no matter which way it is used, and is also detrimental to the patient. Because of this some of our more thoughtful neurologists have given up its use.

We have no right to endeavour to influence other people by the use of our inner forces, even if our object is their good. Each soul has the right to live its life in its own way, and choose for itself either good or evil. That is the object of life, so that each evolving soul should learn wisdom through the lessons learnt as a result of its own mistakes. Far worse is it if others are coerced, not in order to help them, but to defraud them or to make them buy goods they do not require, or sign agreements they would not otherwise put their name to.

One who mis-uses his mental and spiritual powers literally smashes his life up. He works against the laws of life and the universe, and encompasses his own ruin.

There is, however, a far more subtle way of mis-using the mental and spiritual forces than by coercion, mind domination and hetero-suggestion. This method is equally destructive, and if persisted in builds up a painful future. With this method other people are not influenced or dominated, but the finer forces of Nature are coerced by the human will. Mental demands are made on the invisible substance from which, we are told, all things are made, and wealth is compelled to appear. In addition to this, sickness, so it is claimed, is banished, and the invisible forces of life are compelled to operate in such a way as to make life's pathway a bed of roses, without thorns, so that life becomes shorn of all its discipline and experience.

Its devotees "enter the Silence," and there visualize exactly what they think they want, and compel it to appear, in material form, by the strength of their desire or through the exercise of their will.

Some followers of this cult may be able to make an apparent success of it, but I have never yet met any. If they do, however, they will live to regret it, for they are merely practitioners of black magic. Their efforts are of the same nature as sorcery. All such methods build up a heavy debt of future suffering, and seriously hinder the soul in its evolutionary journey.

Entering the Silence is a good thing: it is really entering the inner silence of the soul, the inner sanctuary where the Divine Spirit abides in fulness. To mis-use this inward power for selfish and material ends, and for forcing our human will upon life, so as to make it conform to what *we* think it ought to be is a crime of the first magnitude, which can result only in ultimate failure and disaster.

CHAPTER XIII. OVERCOMING LIMITATIONS AND AWAKENING INWARD POWERS.

Limitations can be overcome through a realization of Truth. When we say this it is taken for granted that every effort will be made on the physical plane. It is necessary to bathe, exercise and breathe fresh air in order to be well: it is equally necessary to work hard, and to give the best of which we are capable, in service, in exchange for that which we receive in the way of supply, if we are to be successful. If you keep a gardener, you must pay him. The money that you pay him is part of what you have earned by the sweat of your brain. Therefore you exchange the work of your brain for the labour of his hands, and you are mutually helped and helpful to one another, both giving and receiving, and each one serving life according to his ability. Taking all this for granted, we will pass on to the metaphysical side of our subject. This, by the way, is vastly the more important, but the outer, practical work is indispensable nevertheless.

In order to overcome limitations it is necessary to know the Truth and to live in the consciousness of It. For instance, if ill-health is our limitation, then, in order to become free it is necessary that we live in the consciousness of the Wholeness of God and His Divine Idea. If our limitation be restricted means, it is necessary that we live in the consciousness of the inexhaustible and unlimited nature of the Substance from which the Creator brings everything into manifestation. If our limitation is disharmony and unhappiness, then we must become attuned to the Divine harmony in such a way and to such an extent as to cause it to be reflected into the outward life. No matter what our limitation may be, we can find liberation and deliverance by looking to our Divine Source, realizing that in the Perfect Reality all our wants are supplied, and then living in the consciousness of this truth.

Ill-health is, apart from physical causes, an outward sign of an inward warfare or disharmony, caused by wrong thoughts, emotions, beliefs and attitude of mind and soul towards life and God. In other words, the life is lived in an "error" consciousness of disease and sickness. First, the inward life has to be adjusted in such a way as to harmonize with the laws of our own being and the Divine purpose of life. There must be an inward surrender to the love principle, after which the thoughts must be brought under control so that health-destroying emotions may no longer impair the health. Further, the whole consciousness must, as often as possible, be raised to a realization of the perfect Wholeness which is the reality. If this course is persevered with, a consciousness of health and wholeness becomes a permanent mental state, with the result that health becomes manifested in the life. The outward life is always a reflection or external manifestation of what we are within, or our state of consciousness. Therefore everything depends upon which kind of consciousness it is in which we live.

One who lives in the mental atmosphere of Divine Wholeness, health and harmony, unconsciously directs all the inner forces of nature into health channels. On the other hand, one who lives in a mental atmosphere of ill-health, as sick and unhealthy people very often do, unconsciously directs all his sub-conscious activities in such a way as to produce sickness and disease.

Again, with regard to lack of means, this state also can be overcome, spiritually, only by living in a higher consciousness of abundance and sufficiency. This affects, unconsciously, every action in such a way as to bring about a better state of affairs. On the other hand, one who lives in a mental atmosphere of limitation and lack, unconsciously directs all his actions towards the production, in his life, of penury and restricted means.

The same rule applies, no matter what the limitations of one's life may be. Freedom can be gained only by realizing the truth about life and being. When we realize the truth, live in the consciousness of it, and become obedient to the laws of life and being, the life becomes increasingly free. This does not mean that if we are plain of feature, and of a stumpy figure, that we shall become beautiful and graceful; but it does mean that these so-called drawbacks will no longer fetter us, and that others will see in us something far better than mere regularity of feature and beauty of form. When the soul is *alive* and the life filled with love, the homeliest face becomes attractive. Neither does it mean that we shall not suffer bereavements and sorrows, difficulties and adversities, but it does mean that we shall cease intensifying these things and creating further troubles by taking life's discipline in the wrong spirit. It also means that we shall be able to overcome all life's difficulties and trials, become a conqueror in the strife, and, in so doing, build up character. Thus the storms of life, instead of destroying us, can succeed only in *making us stronger.* Thus our fate depends not on the storms of life, but upon how we meet them. If we give in to them, or, thinking that they are evil and not a necessary discipline, rebel against them and resist them, then we become shipwrecked on a desolate shore. If, however, we are armed with the knowledge of truth we can set our sails in such a way as to compel the storms of life actually to help us towards the desired haven.

The first step in the direction of knowledge of the truth is right thinking. Every negative thought must be transmuted into its positive opposite,[12] for instance, hate and dislike into love and goodwill, fear into confident trust, poverty into abundance, evil into absolute good, and so on. This will be found to be not easy, but it is possible, and the power to control one's thoughts increases if one perseveres continually, with the passing of the years. A beginner cannot, naturally, expect to be able to exercise the same control as one who has been perseveringly seeking self-mastery for years, but he can make substantial progress and learn from day to day.

The result of thinking in this way is surprising. The reversal of thought may appear at first to be simplicity itself, and to lead nowhere in particular, but after a time the vastness of the subject becomes almost appalling. The cultivation and practice of right thinking gradually lead to a knowledge of the Truth. Not an intellectual knowledge of truth, but a realization, by the soul, of *the* Truth. This is the knowing of the Truth which sets men free. We can then look through all the ages and know that all is well. The heavy burden which has oppressed us so long, rolls from our shoulders, and we become free.

AROUSING INWARD POWERS.

Man is heir to wonderful and illimitable powers, but until he becomes aware of them and consciously identifies himself with them, they lie dormant and unexpressed, and might just as well not exist at all as far as their use to man, in his unawakened state, is concerned. When, however, man becomes awakened to the great truth that he is a spiritual being: when he learns that the little petty self and finite personality are not his real self at all, but merely a mask to the real man: when he realizes that the Spiritual Ego, a true Divine Spark of, or branch or twig of the Eternal Logos,[13] is *his real Self*: when he understands that his body is not himself, that his mind is not himself, that even his soul is not himself, being but vehicles through which he seeks expression, but that he is spirit, deathless, diseaseless, eternal, forming an integral part of the One Spirit and being identical with It, he enters a new life of almost boundless power.

It is unwise to engage in any mystical practices in an attempt to "force" development and unfoldment. Mystic trances are highly dangerous and are also unnecessary. Psychic experiences and the awakening of psychic centres are also dangerous and lead away from our goal. Breathing exercises, whose object is to awaken inward powers, are *highly dangerous* and are to be condemned in consequence. The cultivation of negative passivity such as inhibiting all thought and making oneself quite passive and open to any influence, is also highly dangerous and should be strictly avoided.

In place of all these unwise practices a short time should be set aside each night and also morning, if possible, for getting into touch with Reality. You should then endeavour to realize that the body, mind and soul are but vehicles of expression, mere servants of the true Self or Ego. This will bring about in time, a consciousness of identity with the One Eternal Spirit. What Jesus called "our Father in Heaven."

One might proceed after this fashion: —

"My body is not myself, but is merely something that enables me to live this material life and gain experience.

"My mind is not myself, but merely an instrument which I use and which obeys my will.

"My soul is not myself, but merely a garment of my spirit.

"My will is not myself, but is something of which I, the true Self, make use."

And so on. By this means you gradually approach the great truth which cannot be put into words and which can only become yours through realization or inward spiritual understanding.

In addition one can use a positive statement of Truth, reverently, but with full confidence, such as: "I am a branch in the True Vine."

In course of time you will become possessed of a feeling of tremendous and unlimited power and security. This is a great responsibility for this power must be used only in service and not for selfish purposes. If it is used for the acquisition of wealth and the gaining of temporal power, great disaster will be the inevitable result. Yet, if used aright, it is bound to have a great, though unconscious, influence for good on the life, and for this you are not responsible. Constantly endeavour to serve and bless others, then, because you do not seek them, crowds of blessings will come into your life unbidden, great happiness being one of the chief. Having found the kingdom of heaven it will be your experience that all needed good will be added unto you.

This power may also be used to strengthen character, to overcome in the conflicts of the soul, and to build up the spiritual body which will be our vehicle of expression in higher realms.

Footnotes

1.   The powers of the sub-conscious mind are dealt with in other chapters. The Powers of the Spirit are far greater and finer than those of the sub-conscious mind.

2.   This subject is dealt with in "The Path of Victory" by the same author, and published by The Science of Thought Press.

3.   In addition to the "fate" or "future" which every thought and action builds, there is, behind all evolution, a gigantic plan. This wonderful plan that embraces all, from the stupendous conception of a limitless universe down to the smallest electron, is being worked out through the ages with absolute precision. Nothing can prevent this plan from being brought into manifestation. It gathers up our past and weaves it into our present life, just in the same way that it is busily gathering up our present life and weaving it into future fate. It works it all into the big plan, somehow, and with infinite skill. The plan is bound to be followed (this, too, is fate) but HOW we follow it, either with willingness and happiness, or opposition or woe, rests with us (this is free will).

4.   Another cause is that the soul has failed to learn certain lessons, therefore, in this life, many painful experiences are brought to bear, in such a way, as to teach the necessary lessons. The lessons are, however, learnt only if painful or unpleasant experiences are met in the right way. So long as man believes that he is unjustly treated by fate and that he does not "deserve" what life metes out to him, he intensifies his troubles, both now and hereafter, through not learning the lessons that life desires to teach. When, however man realizes and admits that life is just and that the cause of all his troubles is within himself, he, like the prodigal son comes to himself and, soon afterwards, begins his homeward journey. Yet another cause is that the soul is deficient in character. Strength and stability of character can be built up through the soul meeting trouble and difficulty. Again it must be pointed out that they must be met in the right spirit.

5.   This is the inner secret of all esoteric teaching. The new birth, or regeneration, means the awakening of the soul to conscious immortality. The old self, that was bound to the wheel of fate and the plane of cause and effect from which it could never free itself, owing to the fact that it was continually binding itself to the wheel afresh, through following selfish desires, dies, and a new self is born. In other words, the consciousness is raised from the plane of sin and death, of sensuality and desire, of restriction and captivity, to the higher plane of Spirit, where man realizes that he is a son of God. He discovers that the Divine Spark within is his true self. He realizes also that he has always lived-in his real Spiritual Self. Beginning and end, like change and decay, belong purely to the material plane and have no place in Reality. They form part of this present three dimensional existence but have no reality. Endless being is the reality. Anything short of this is mere illusion. It is not necessary, therefore, to believe in the theory of reincarnation or that all our experiences must of necessity take place on this plane. Sufficient to know that we can never die, that we cannot escape from ourselves, and that to neglect seeking with all our heart for union once again with our Divine Source, is merely to prolong our sufferings.

6.   It must not be deduced from this that the author deprecates large achievement. There must always be the few who have to bear huge responsibilities. The real success of the lives of these great ones depends entirely upon their MOTIVE. If they seek merely power, fame and self-aggrandisement, then their life, no matter how it may APPEAR otherwise, can be only a failure. If, however, their motive is SERVICE, then their life is truly successful, no matter how it may appear to be otherwise.

7.   For a fuller explanation of this metaphysical statement see Science of Thought Text Books, Nos. I. and II.

8.   See also "The Power of Thought" by the same author, published by The Science of Thought Press, Chichester.

9.   This may seem, at first sight, to be a sweeping statement, but two homely illustrations will prove its reasonableness. First we will take the case of a man committed to prison for law-breaking. His environment is obviously due to his wrong actions, the latter being the offspring of his thoughts, for all actions spring from thoughts. Next let us take the case of a man who is the trusted head of an efficient business. Obviously his position is the result of his actions, for he has climbed to it by hard work and faithful service, all due in the first place to constructive thinking and a right attitude of mind.

10.   See also "The Fundamentals of True Success," by the same author and published by The Science of Thought Press, Chichester.

11.   This subject is treated fully in "The Fundamentals of True Success," by the same author. Published by The Science of Thought Press, Chichester.

12.   See also "The Power of Thought" and "The Way of Escape," by the same author and publisher.

13.   "I am the Vine, ye are the branches." —Jesus.